BEYOND THE BOX

JOAN KALIFF

TABLE OF CONTENTS

"The moments that shaped me weren't moments of clarity, but moments of chaos. They weren't moments of refinement, but moments of reckoning. They were pressure points that pushed me to my limits, forcing me to adapt and evolve. In the midst of uncertainty and turmoil, I discovered my resilience, my strength, and my true self. These moments of unclarity molded me into the person I am today, and I'm grateful for the struggle."

The compelling argument, the story. To write, or not to write. Why dig up a past better forgotten, I thought. I mean, the story, my story, it isn't a pretty one. The triumphs weren't worth the trials. The lessons were just lessons. There was no reward for the work or retribution for the injustice. There was nothing. Just a story full of indifference and depth full of definition.

F(story) = (intensity + grip) - (triumphs - trials) + (lessons - reward) - (retribution - injustice) = (indifference + depth + definition)

Life has always had a way of getting my attention. Existing, being, it's more work than you'd think. I've traveled some distances but in order to understand space, I'd have to understand indifference. I'd have to backtrack. Return to a moment better left alone.

$$\text{Indifference Formula: } I = (D - U) / S$$

> I = Indifference
> D = Distance traveled
> U = Understanding of space
> S = Sensitivity to the passage of time

OPPOSITES ATTRACT

My father was a very close-minded person. He grew up with a specific set of beliefs that were both religious and unkind. On the other hand, my mother was the complete opposite. She had an open mind and showed love to everyone. She went through hell for being herself.

$$(\text{Sensitivity} = (EI \times EV) / ES)$$

My Father : A double-edged sword. Emotions like an inferno, blazing out of control, consuming everything in his path.

My Mother: A love that knew no bounds, endlessly she gave. She embodied an unwavering affection toward everyone.

FORCE OF ATTRACTION:

Attached to an idea, its force propels forward, resonating a frequency that vibrates through existence like a tuning fork responding to a matching sound. Surrounded, overwhelmed by thoughts and emotions. Their energy flows through my veins, leaving me distracted and stimulated.

The gravity of an idea, a compelling force matching a planet's gravitational pull. Surrendering to an idea is like embracing fate, offering both freedom and fear. Becoming a vessel. Transforming noise into music. Mirroring the shift from chaos to order The force's dance echoes particle behavior with wave-particle duality, blurring the lines between particles and waves.

FORMULA FOR THE FORCE OF ATTRACTION:

$$F = (GMm) / r^2$$

F: Force of attraction
G: Gravitational constant (6.674 × 10^-11 N m^2 / kg^2)
M: Mass of the first object
m: Mass of the second object
r: Distance between the centers of the two objects.

$$F = m * a$$
Force equals mass times acceleration

Fast Forward : I could tell you about the time the police had the house surrounded and the roads closed off. They were trying to negotiate my fathers surrender over their megaphone. I could tell you about the time both my parents left us alone and went out on the dirt bike to get some more booze. They were gone for about 6 hours and returned home all cut up and bleeding, talking about almost becoming a sacrifice and how they got away. I could tell you about the guy who used to break into our house. He used to climb in my bedroom window, and over my head. I could tell you about the Highway killer, and the encounter we had with him. I could tell you a story about a shower killer. A drug cartel out in the middle of the desert. And even about being kidnapped, drugged, raped, and sold. I've been hit by the car, and dragged down the road. But I'll start with simpler days. Back to my earliest memory.

I learned something in **1986**, my father had a peculiar talent for misplacing everything he touched. When he began drinking, his forgetfulness escalated, and he would invariably lose track of various items. In response to his misplaced possessions, he would become enraged and start yelling, often accusing someone of taking them. To put an end to the yelling, I would try to track them down for him. Sometimes it took a significant amount of time, while on other occasions, I simply retraced his last steps, which invariably led to the missing. It was a process that not only gave me a sense of purpose and control, but also became an escape.

The missing, the hidden, there was a difference. Nothing was missing in his life. If anything, everything ran as far and as fast as possible, never looking back. I did, and it was the hardest thing I ever did but I wanted to forget that girl. I wanted to forget that life. I wanted to pretend it didn't exist and I was somebody else. An orphan, a wanderer, just the girl next door. (**X - Y → X - Y**)

CHEMICAL REACTION X - Y → X - Y:
- Reactants: X - Y (compound of elements X and Y).
- Products: X - Y (another compound of elements X and Y).
- Chemical change: Combination, decomposition, or other reactions.
- Stoichiometry: Balanced chemical equation shows moles or molecules.
- Reaction conditions: Temperature, pressure, and catalyst affect rate and outcome.
- Equilibrium: Some reactions reach a state of equilibrium (forward and reverse reactions occur at the same rate).
- Applications: Synthesis, industry, environment, analytical chemistry, biological processes.

(FOCAL POINT GAP FORMULA)

Distance between focal points = 2 * (Distance between objects) / (1 - (Magnification))

Growing up, my father constantly criticized me, always finding fault in my actions. His anger towards me only seemed to escalate when I responded with laughter instead of fear. He believed my words were a source of trouble, but I quickly realized that his violence was inevitable, regardless of what I said. To him, there were only absolutes - right, wrong, and indifferent - equating to smart, stupid, and incompetent, with him always claiming the role of the intelligent one. His prejudice and rage fueled his actions, leading to relentless physical abuse whenever I provoked him, leaving me bruised and broken. Despite the pain, he never stopped until he felt satisfied, demonstrating his power over me with each strike of the belt. His actions instilled in me a twisted understanding of power dynamics, shaping the way I would navigate similar situations in the future.

When I look through the magnifying glass, I observe a mix. A contrast in viewpoints - some enlarged, others reduced. A fusion of plenty and nothing, producing a misleading sight.

I became familiar with the story at a young age. It revolved around the constant interplay of animosity. Unfortunately, it permeated in every single part of the picture.

Our house had a lack of affection. Well, unless hate was attention. I don't know how many times I was dragged out from hiding and beaten. Maybe I didn't go home the way I went to school. Maybe I was five minutes late, my dad knew the route. Maybe I didn't speak up when spoken to. In our house there was no love, but there were plenty of rules.. (Imprisoned, I was confined to an idea that didn't move. Go beyond a room.)

In the shadows of our abode, A chilling wind of hate flowed.
A place void of affection's embrace, Where fear held every corner's space.
A child, with a heart quivering in dread, Dragged from hiding, seeing red.
Each step a torturous journey led, Bruises and wounds that no one read.
The way to school, a path well-known, Became a battlefield of wails and moans.
A tardy arrival, a fateful sin, Her route, a trap he'd surely win.
A sanctuary meant for peace and rest, Transformed into a place of unrest.
A soul yearning for warmth and grace, In the cruel confines of that dark place. . .

CHAOS FORMULA:

[Lack of order] + [Surprises] + [Unpredictability] -> [Heightened awareness] + [Adaptation] + [Growth]

The chaos formula summarizes the transformation from a state of disorder and uncertainty to a state of increased awareness, adaptability, and growth. It commences with the components of "lack of order" (random events, unpredictable circumstances), "surprises" (unexpected occurrences), and "unpredictability" (unknown outcomes). The introduction of the elements of "embracing the chaos" and "seeking understanding" represents the choice to confront the chaos rather than resist it.

Resistance, a word that didn't exist in our house. The problem, I was the force counteracting the flow of the current in that house and my father knew it.

$$R = V/I$$

R is resistance in ohms (Ω)
V is voltage in volts (V)
I is current in amperes (A)

Despite facing brutal beatings, I repeatedly resisted. The consequences were harsh and varied, from boots and belts to ashtrays and whatever else that man could get his hands on. Nevertheless, I refused to yield, stay silent, or stand submissive. I wasn't made that way. I was made to stand up and face fear for what it was. Nothing but a moment made to pass just like everything else. I mean, after all, that's how I was raised. To stand, to take a beating. And to take the beating as many times as it took until I wasn't the one taking the beating anymore.

We lived in a house where a man was creating soldiers. Soldiers that would stand, challenge, and one day destroy him. I wasn't the one to kill the man. I emancipated myself when I was 15 and ran away from that life. There were those first few years I missed the old though. I was struggling with the adjustments. Quiet was too silent. I suppose when life got easy I made it hard. I think I made it hard because I was used to the hard way. The hard way was the only way I knew. An old song I grew up listening to. When I think back on the roads I've gone down and come from, I ask why? Why I chose them to begin with. But then again, not all roads walked down look bad in the beginning.

With this book, I didn't want it to be a biography, but I didn't really want to go into the pieces, parts, and mechanics. The order of operations. There was no order in my life so why try to make it fit in a book. Instead I chose to share some of the adventures and misfortunes of those roads. Life in the In-Between.

THE SUMMER OF 87

On a sun-kissed day, while my parents celebrated, we piled into my father's Camaro and set off towards Westport. Our destination was my mother's sister's house. Although I'm not privy to the details of their conversation, I noticed that my uncle appeared visibly upset. During our visit, my aunt Joan captured a moment with a photograph of my little sister and me. Unfortunately, my sister had an accident and wet her pants. I suppose it was a familiar situation for me, but it seemed to be a new experience for her.

After a brief stay, we were instructed to return to the car and head back home. Not long after we arrived home, we heard the voices of police officers coming from a megaphone. We rushed to the open window and looked out. Coggeshall Street was blocked off on all four sides, preventing any traffic from passing through. From our third-story window, I witnessed the officers attempting to persuade my father to surrender.

My father while driving was so drunk he swerved and hit a car. It was the reason my sister wet her pants. She was afraid. The pregnant female was injured in the accident.

1988, There are certain dates that leave an unforgettable imprint in your mind. One such date happened during an ordinary evening stroll with my mother and brother, David. Our destination was the liquor store down the street, a quick errand to replenish our father's dwindling supply of booze. The shortcut through Kenyon Street had been traversed countless times before, but this particular night held an eerie and unsettling atmosphere. We walked down the dark and unlit street, my mother noticed a figure standing off in the distance, away from the road. Despite the darkness, it was clear that someone was there, but we couldn't make out any details. My intoxicated mother, oblivious to the unfolding scene ahead of her, began walking towards the figure. My brother, sensing something amiss, repeatedly asked her to leave. However, her inebriated state prevented her from comprehending the situation. We followed close behind as my mother stumbled forward, drawn towards the enigmatic figure in the darkness.

In a state of limp unresponsiveness, the woman laid as mom frantically tried to rouse her by shaking her. The man drew closer with each step, his face inches from my mother's. As he came closer, we noticed shades of blue tinting her skin and a chilling emanation from her body. In a moment of quick thinking, my brother grabbed her arm, and we sprinted back home to get my dad. My sister, following his instructions, called the police. Although drunk, they were not mindless of the situation. However, when my father returned to the scene of the incident, there was no one in sight. There was nothing there. The police took down the few details my mom could give but she was drunk.

A few days later a woman's body was found on the overpass we were under when we stumbled upon her a few nights earlier.

Between 1988 and 1989, an unidentified serial killer known as the New Bedford Highway Killer committed several murders in New Bedford, Massachusetts. The victims were primarily sex workers or individuals struggling with addiction. Authorities believe that the killer may have assaulted additional women, but the exact number remains unknown.

1989, it was a turning point in history.

April 28,1989, the day that would follow me for the rest of my life. We lived on County Street. In a little house on the corner. My father had a girlfriend and that made my mother mad. One night my parents were drinking and partying with their friend when things got out of hand. My mother confronted her and slapped her in the face. Of course she got up, grabbed her bag and started walking home. She only lived a block over. And my mother followed. Of course my older sister, brother, and I all followed. My mother took out a knife and slashed her tires. She picked up some cans and started smashing the windows. I don't know who threw paint all over the car but I know my sister told the police it was her when they asked. We were in the basement pretending to be painting when they arrived. They called us upstairs to ask us about the incident. My brother and I kept our mouths shut when the police insisted we tell them who vandalized the car. That's when my sister came up the stairs and told them she did it. We got a summons to appear in court. It went to trial but I had a warrant out for my arrest because my Dad raped my sister and ran off to New Mexico. You know my mom would follow. I was 10 years old.

1986,87,88, and 89, they were the four years that would shape my entire life.

In 86, I spent a significant amount of time at the beach, enjoying the company of my father and going to church. My mother would often pack a lunch for us or meet my father during his lunch break. Occasionally, my grandfather would come over to supervise me, and we would embark on can collection outings, followed by lunch at a soup kitchen. As a reward, I was permitted to visit the penny candy shop on our way back and spend twenty-five cents, which would yield a substantial amount of candy. At the age of seven, I experienced a sense of pure joy and contentment.

Church was a source of joy for me. My father, aware of my fondness for it, would sometimes use it as a form of punishment, keeping me away as a consequence. Victory Baptist Church, where Pastor Barrett, a kind man with two daughters, ministered, became a significant part of my life. I developed a close relationship with the family and was frequently invited to join them for dinners or sleepovers. I also spent considerable time in Sunday school with my teacher, visiting her home and engaging in various activities such as lunch outings or miniature golf.

My father, a remarkable man, was my ultimate hero when I was seven years old. His presence was a magnet that drew me wherever he went. Whenever he allowed me to tag along, I eagerly followed him. Our destinations included liquor stores, bars, and occasional visits to friends or family when he was drinking. Liquor stores offered a particular delight—the candy. With just a dollar, I could get two bags, presenting a plethora of delectable options that filled me with joy. Bars held a different charm. There, I would sit, content with a pickle the size of my hand, listening to the melodious tunes of the jukebox as my father and his friends engaged in conversation and played pool.

In '87, I witnessed a lot. From our window, we watched my mom being assaulted, we shouted for them to stop, but nobody was listening. I remember watching the woman's boyfriend trip my mom, but they fought dirty. When he tripped my mom, she fell, and the girl got on top of her and began hitting her head against the ground. My father, who was drunk, stood by and casually talked to the attacker's partner as if nothing was happening at all. She wrongly accused my mother of being involved with her boyfriend, who happened to be my father's enemy; yet my father acted like they were best friends that night.

That was also the year my parents disappeared for like 6 hours. They had a dirt bike and were running real fast to the liquor store. They left my older sister in charge, who was around nine or ten years old at the time. When they finally came back, we rushed downstairs to greet them. To our shock, they were covered in blood.

They explained that they had been pursued and almost sacrificed, but fortunately managed to escape.

So many things happened that year. That was also the year my father ran that poor pregnant woman off the road.

That was the year my brother had his first girlfriend too. He was only eight years old and she happened to be our next-door neighbor. Her mother was a hospital employee who worked long days so you'd often find her daughter outside with my sister and brother. One evening, my sister was invited to sleep over at their house and I was kindly included by the girl-friend's mother. During the sleepover, we ended up having a pillow fight which unfortunately did not impress her mother who was working at the hospital that night. In the midst of the playful chaos, I accidentally punc-tured her eardrum and as a result, my brother's brief relationship came to an end.

88, that was the year my feelings toward my father started changing. One day I forgot to unroll my bell bottoms when I walked through the door. When I walked in my father started yelling, I ran under the bed and he dragged me out. He took off his belt and left me screaming. He held my arm so I couldn't move, and he kept on whaling.

That was the year we came face to face with a Serial Killer. And the year my dad would go into hiding.

He was being sought by the authorities for his involvement in my sister's sexual assault. My mother was hiding him out. One of the stipulations to my sister returning was that he was not allowed in the house. I recall the social worker frequently visiting our living room, checking to ensure he wasn't present. We would eavesdrop on their discussions through the vent while sitting in the basement. My mom said my father ran off, and my sister returned home, but my father never left.

That was the year he stayed in hiding. He'd hide out during the day but when all those government buildings closed down for the evening, he'd crack a bar, and sit there partying.

I don't know how many times my sister was molested that year. I remember being sent to my room and not feeling comfortable being upstairs alone. We had an intruder who broke in all the time. He'd come through my bedroom window when I slept. I was afraid so I'd sit by the vent. I was always sent to my room when dad sent mom to the store with my brother. My father was trying to bribe her with candy and food. He was trying to touch her and she was telling him no. My mother walked through the door and asked why I was in bed? I think my mother knew that night that something wasn't right . She didn't leave her alone after that.

Mom was protective of us, but dad, I don't know how many times she saved me from him. I always got the beatings. My father was touching my sister, and when it came to my brother, he was like the prodigal son. Neither one of them were getting an ass whooping.

88 was rough with everything going on. We were barely going to school. My parents were always drunk. And that was the year of the intruder constantly in the house. There were a few nights my parents were so drunk they left the man to wander the house. He was in the basement or the entry hall. Sometimes he'd climb through my mother's sun room, or through my bedroom window. There was that one night though. The night my father heard someone walking around upstairs. We were asleep in bed when my father woke us with his voice. He was asking us to come into the hallway. My brother couldn't get out of bed. That man was in his room. He jumped out the window real fast when my father chased after him with an ax. Time went on and this was our normal. Dad was in hiding and we had an intruder.

89, not only a year that would change my life in the long run, but a year that would change everything forever. That was the year my father decided to run to New Mexico. He left my mom behind and took my brother with him. We had an intruder, and nobody to protect us. My mom had us sleeping on the floor in the living room. We'd usually sleep in front of the doors. Sometimes you'd hear a doorknob jiggle and you knew he was in the house. By the time the police arrived, he was always gone. He'd go out the same way he came in.

My father had pulled a scheme for quick money before he left. He faked a fall and they settled out of court. My mother was waiting on that check for a few months. The money finally arrived and we followed my father to New Mexico. I remember the day we left. We packed a few things and left everything behind. My mom called a taxi and it drove us to the bus station. We sat on that bus for two and a half days.

Upon our arrival in New Mexico, we were greeted by my father and brother. We then proceeded to my aunt's residence, which was a small studio apartment. She lived there with her boyfriend, son, his girlfriend, their children, as well as my dad, brother, and us. Unfortunately, the living conditions were less than desirable as the studio was dilapidated, unclean, and plagued with cockroaches.

1989 goes into 1990.

1990, that was a scene out of a movie.

It was a beautiful day. My brother and I made a ramp. It wouldn't hold our weight though and kept falling so we were looking for something stronger to hold the board. I was on the bike doing a test run when a swat vehicle pulled up, cruisers surrounded the house, and the police came out of nowhere.

I don't know what happened to my parents that day, but I know what happened to us. I was in a foreign place. I don't think I ate anything but burgers when I did eat. And I was only given burgers because I wouldn't eat. I wouldn't eat for days. I just wanted to go home. I was placed with my sister but she resented me and I was moved. I hated her. My life was horrible because of her. She didn't want to be home but I did.

One of us had to leave and I was the more difficult one. I had lead poisoning my whole life. My mom knew what to do and had my medicine but it did me no good that night. I was rushed to the hospital but I guess in all the commotion I hurt another resident and she didn't feel comfortable with me there. I left the following morning.

I moved around a lot in 1990. From shelter to shelter waiting for something long term. My older brother and sister went to a group home, and my little brother and sisters went to foster homes. Me, I had nothing, I was 10 years old in a foreign world.

I had nothing but time. Time to watch time pass by. I waited and hoped, but when that didn't work, I began to flee. There was a sense of uncertainty. I was facing too many problems on my own. Even when I was taken in by a foster family. My foster siblings were rigid and unfriendly. I didn't want to be around those who judged me, so I left. When I was caught, I was sent to Nambe Falls. That didn't last long. In the midst of winter, I escaped. The ground was blanketed with snow. I endured hours in the freezing cold. Of course I got caught so I waited. When warmer temperatures arrived, I ran away again.

I had a problem making my bed. Every time I made it, the staff would strip it. I didn't crease the corners before the tuck. I didn't leave a quarter inch between the fold. I was being punished and I didnt even do anything wrong. I just wanted 1987 back. I wanted my parents. I wanted to go home. And it's where the police always found me. My parents always turned me in. They'd get a call saying I was on my way. And when I arrived the police were waiting.

This went on for a while. My file was growing but not for anything good. I had a reputation as a runaway child. There were hundreds of discussions and notes documented. Somebody intervened though, it was decided that I would join my brother and sister at the Jemez House.

I was eleven going on 12 and it was 1991 going on 1992

The Jemez House, home for a little while. My first week there the counselor was fired. I showed up at the Christmas party inebriated. We toasted my arrival.

The staff, well, I had my favorites, but we all did. Keith and Dennis brought me to my family visits. And Eleanor was just the sweetest. She'd take me just about anywhere I wanted to go. Eppie, he was the one always chasing me. He'd pack us all up in the van and bring us to church. Eva, we all made fun of, but there was just something dark about that woman. Isabel in the kitchen, a culinary queen. And Ida on the phone but that woman was a machine. When it came to the kids, we got along for the most part, and if we didn't we just took it into the bathrooms. We were kids, we had all the answers. Because we had all the answers, you know we got in trouble.

I was always running away from that place. I don't know where I was going or what I was thinking but I ended up in a detention center, on probation, and on my way to YDDC. (what do you expect to happen when you put a low risk individual with a high risk individual? 1 of 2 things happens. Either one of you walks, or one of you changes. The result becomes the consequence. I was packing my things up and waiting to be transported to YDDC when my brother and sister started begging me to just go to school. Faced with the prospect of several years in juvie, I knew my life was about to change. I gathered my belongings, stepped into the van, and we drove off. As we passed by my school, a sudden opportunity arose. Someone intervened, and the van pulled up in front of the school's doors, offering me a last chance to choose a different path. By the time school ended, my efforts had paid off. I was honored with multiple certificates. It turned out that I had become the student with the most significant improvement. I stayed out of trouble and finished my probation. Then I ran away again.

Out of the 1,471,200 juvenile delinquency cases processed in 1992, 60% involved juveniles under 16 years of age. At the time, I was 12 years old and easily influenced. Due to my lack of knowledge, I found myself in some problematic situations.

In 2009, the Juvenile Justice Services/Facilities (JJS) adopted the Cambiar New Mexico model, shifting the focus from confinement and punishment to rehabilitation and regionalization.

1992, a year of reckless pursuits. The amount of times I ran away. You'd think I'd learn my lesson, but I didn't. At this point my entire family was reckless. My brother and sister had run away from the Jemez House and my parents were hiding them out. Thanksgiving morning my brother, sister, and I were all hiding on the roof. We were watching the police search the duplex. We lived on Onate street at the time. I had a few relatives renting out the adjacent apartments. My younger brother ran as soon as his foster fathers brought him to the house. He came up to the roof with us and we waited til they left. My father said we'd have to turn ourselves in but we didn't. We went to work at the car wash under the table. That was a tragic story in itself. My mother was having an affair and my father found out. I was with her and stayed hidden when she got caught. My father put her in intensive care for a while. I stayed on the run and ended up at a homeless shelter with my uncle. That lasted for a few weeks when the police found me. They came in and surrounded the place. I was walking to my uncle's room from the office when I was grabbed and put in the back of a police car. The detective drove down the road and met up with his partner who had my little brother in the back of the car. We were transported to a locked facility.

Heights Psychiatric Hospital, a place I couldn't escape, but that didn't mean I wouldn't try. A year and a half behind plexiglass windows and locked doors. Following orders, taking the pills I was given, and agreeing with everything the doctors said. It was the only way I would get out of the place. I had to learn how to play a game. I started telling them what they wanted to hear and pretended to change. It bought me my freedom too.

A.W.O.L / ABSENT WITHOUT LEAVE

It was either absent or angry.

In total alignment with the popular statement of " being on ones own agenda", Joan is the epitome of this phrase. She frequently refuses to actively participate in the daily routine of our program, but yet cannot understand why disciplinary measures are taken.

Recommendations; A long term residential treatment center. The RTC should be a level 3 or 4 facility. The focus of treatment should be restructuring Joan based on her unusually abusive home situation.

This child's history of abuse and neglect is so severe that a well- defended personality was her only survival tactic.

Expectation; that Joan begins to deteriorate as she is able to trust. Because Joan's home is so abusive, her reporting may take on a tone that is difficult to believe. However, the reporting is neither hystionic nor unconfirmed.

The patient does not seem to be an aggressive child. It seems her high motor activity level is non- purposeful behavior rather than aggressive behavior.

She certainly is a very intelligent girl with a good vocabulary and knows how to make her point forcefully.

Given the fact that she had not been stabilized in five placements prior to her arrival here, we feel that she has developed a significant amount of trust in our staff, our therapist, and in some of our residents.

Joan is well documented in her crusade in not completing tasks. While it is touching to see her resist in order to play, she must nevertheless understand the relevance of completing her assigned tasks. desired goal : Increase Joan's work contribution on the ranch.

In summary, we are pleased that Joan is no longer running away from her problems, and we look forward to helping her cope with some very critical issues.

In 1993, upon my arrival at the Los Alamos Girls Ranch, I was given some freedom to explore within the boundaries of the rules. I attended school and became involved in the theater community, finding success. However, my family contacted me and informed me that my uncle was in the area with my brother and wanted to see me. In order to meet them, I told the staff that I was going to the store, but instead ran away. The next day, my parents turned me in and the ranch rejected me. As a result, I ended up at a shelter where I had been numerous times before. Once the intake process was over, I quickly escaped.

When not confined to a facility, I was constantly evading capture. My days were spent roaming the streets under the cover of darkness, meticulously avoiding main streets and public places to remain undetected.

Living on the run meant leaving behind everything familiar. My routine was constantly changing, and I lost contact with the people I knew. I became a phantom, off the radar of everyone. The question "Where's Joan?" echoed through my daily life, with my parents, the police, friends, and even the Department of Children, Youth, and Families searching for me.

After enduring so much because of adults, it was difficult for me to trust them. During the daytime, I would wander through town near the mountainside, trying to remain unnoticed. As night fell, I would venture into the streets, seeking trouble and attending parties. My life was a cycle of evading authorities and immersing myself in the chaos of the night.

At times, I would hop around from one house to another as I made new acquaintances who were willing to shelter me until the area became unsafe. I often found myself in the company of individuals facing longer prison sentences than myself. I started associating with the offspring of gang members and leaders of drug cartels. Regrettably, I placed an unwarranted trust in these people.

I received an invitation to a party one night. I developed a liking for one of the boys, so I informed a friend that I would be attending. Despite my friend's efforts to dissuade me and her concern about my going alone, I was determined to go. (East Side Party) I lived in the West Side

As I entered the room, it felt like a dramatic movie scene. The music blared and there were people indulging in smoking, drinking, and engaging in romantic encounters. However, this was not my kind of environment. I was labeled as a tease and ultimately asked to leave because I refused to engage in sexual activities.

Two of the men seized me while a third unlatched the window. In no time, they had me held by my limbs and were swinging me back and forth. I struggled and thrashed until I broke free. Making a quick escape, I dashed out the door, crossed the street, and took off through the hills. Catching sight of headlights on the road, I raced further into the rugged terrain.

As I approached the gas station a few miles away, I noticed it illuminated in the distance. My immediate goal was to reach it before I was caught.

Luckily, I made it just in time. Once inside, I requested the cashier to help me find a cab. He could sense something was off as he observed a car pulling up and men exiting it. They entered the store, glanced at me, and headed to the cooler for some drinks. Sensing danger, the cashier instructed me to stand behind the counter which I did obediently. He had his hand on the emergency button as they approached to pay for their items.

After making their payment, they left and began mocking us. The taxi arrived, but I had no destination or funds to cover the fare. I recalled a friend mentioning her location, so I instructed the taxi to take me there. Upon arrival, I attempted to flee because I lacked the means to pay. However, I was caught as I headed towards the hotel room the cab driver watched. The cab driver knocked on the door and insisted on receiving payment or he would involve law enforcement.

I was not familiar with the individual in that room, he settled the bill in order to evade the authorities. As a result, I found myself stranded in the desert for a period of time with the candy man.

(I always had a way of going from bad to worse. And each situation I put myself in could have gotten me killed.)

Amidst the countless encounters I experienced, each individual story seemed insignificant. Every person I encountered posed unique challenges that demanded my attention and response. Perhaps my trust was excessive, as I persistently sought something deeper and more meaningful. This pursuit may have led me into various challenging situations, but as time progressed, so did I, evolving and learning from these experiences.

(Numerous unnecessary wars resulted from the substantial resistance encountered by each experience from all parties involved.)

Throughout my life, I've been in a constant state of absence, unsure whether I was fleeing from an unknown force or pursuing an elusive goal. I suppose that's about the time that I began to question concepts and ideas that went beyond traditional reasoning, believing that this was the only way to understand a life of purpose and meaning.

In my pursuit of a goal, I encountered numerous obstacles and challenges designed to discourage me. The path was fraught with difficulties, and I often felt tempted to succumb to defeat. However, deep within me, a persistent voice urged me to persevere. That voice empowered me to speak up, giving birth to a new idea.

The ideas lacked substance, consisting of mere words or rudimentary frameworks without a solid foundation. Instead of developing the concepts behind these ideas, I dedicated my life to comprehending them. From their core to their outermost layers, the pieces, parts, and components that define them. These ideas were shaped by human-crafted rules and laws, accompanied by underlying observations. While we may grasp the written words, we fail to fully comprehend their deeper meanings.

Instead of the adult teaching the child, I encountered rudimentary thinking, cognitive limitations, mental shortcuts, and a lack of education. The rigid and biased thinking, along with the one-way paths and dead ends I was directed down, resulted in a significant investment of time and effort in understanding and grasping concepts.

THE PURSUIT OF MEANING FRAMEWORK

Phase 1: Awareness
1.1 Recognition: Identify limitations of traditional reasoning
1.2 Reflection: Examine personal beliefs and assumptions
1.3 Re-evaluation: Challenge established concepts and ideas

Phase 2: Questioning
2.1 Inquiry: Ask fundamental questions about life and meaning
2.2 Analysis: Examine evidence and arguments for and against
2.3 Synthesis: Integrate new information into existing knowledge

Phase 3: Exploration
3.1 Investigation: Seek out diverse perspectives and sources
3.2 Experimentation: Test ideas and hypotheses through experience
3.3 Iteration: Refine understanding through continuous learning

Phase 4: Perseverance
4.1 Resilience: Develop coping strategies for obstacles and setbacks
4.2 Adaptability_l: Embrace change and uncertainty
4.3 Motivation: Cultivate inner drive and purpose

Phase 5: Insight
5.1 Integration: Connect new understanding to daily life
5.2 Application: Put insights into practice
5.3 Evaluation: Assess progress and adjust course as needed

THE PURSUIT OF MEANING FORMULA

$$M = (A \times Q) + (E \times P) + I$$

    Where:
        M = Meaning
        A = Awareness (recognition, reflection, re-evaluation)
        Q = Questioning (inquiry, analysis, synthesis)
        E = Exploration (investigation, experimentation, iteration)
        P = Perseverance (resilience, adaptability, motivation)
        I = Insight (integration, application, evaluation)

KEY PRINCIPLES:
1. Embrace curiosity and skepticism
2. Challenge assumptions and conventions
3. Seek depth over breadth in knowledge
4. Cultivate resilience and adaptability
5. Integrate new insights into daily life

APPLICATION:
1. Personal Growth: Apply the framework to personal struggles and aspirations
2. Critical Thinking: Use the formula to evaluate information and ideas
3. Innovation: Employ the framework to develop novel solutions
4. Education: Integrate the principles into learning and teaching

Before his downfall, even the devil was regarded as pure and holy.

In religious discussions, we often focus on figures like Jesus, the devil, prophets, and saints, but rarely consider the reasons behind their significance. The inherent evils of humanity, passed down from one person to another, contribute to this understanding. Adam and Eve's disobedience in the Garden of Eden, along with 人类's altruistic and self-centered instincts, have shaped these qualities as essential for survival.

According to human interpretation of religious texts, God instructed Abraham to sacrifice his only son, Joseph. However, it was not Joseph who was sacrificed; instead, God sacrificed Jesus. Joseph was spared, while Jesus was not, as depicted in Genesis chapters 12-25.

Rudimentary thinking, akin to solving a Rubik's cube, may explain why challenges have persisted throughout history.

Between Joseph's time (circa 1700-1600 BCE) and Jesus' era (approximately 4 BCE to 30 CE), cognitive and critical thinking skills were not as highly valued or developed as they are in contemporary society.

In ancient societies, thinking was heavily influenced by myths, traditions, religious and political authorities, and personal experiences, leading to a prevalence of cognitive biases, superstitions, and dogmatic beliefs. Critical thinking, as we know it today, is a relatively recent development, tracing its roots to ancient Greece and Rome and further refined during the Enlightenment and scientific revolutions. The gradual evolution of cognitive and critical thinking abilities has been shaped by the spread of education and literacy, scientific discoveries and empirical methods, philosophical inquiry and skepticism, and cultural exchange and diversity. These factors have fostered the development of analytical and rational thinking skills, promoted critical evaluation and logical reasoning, encouraged questioning and examination of assumptions, and broadened cognitive horizons, leading to the gradual shift from mythological, traditional, authoritarian, and intuitive thinking to the critical, analytical, and evidence-based thinking that characterizes modern societies.

Throughout history, numerous notable individuals have played a pivotal role in advancing critical thinking and cognitive abilities. In ancient Greece, Socrates, Plato, and Aristotle laid the groundwork for philosophical inquiry, challenging assumptions and promoting intellectual curiosity.

In ancient India, Buddha and Charvaka questioned traditional beliefs and encouraged skepticism. During the medieval period, Thomas Aquinas integrated philosophy with Christian theology, while William of Ockham emphasized simplicity and empirical evidence. The Enlightenment era saw the rise of René Descartes, John Locke, and Immanuel Kant, who further developed critical thinking through their ideas on skepticism, empiricism, and reason. These influential thinkers, among many others, have contributed to the evolution of critical thinking and cognitive skills, leaving a lasting impact on the intellectual landscape throughout history.

Time is a neutral measure of change and progression, while evil is a human construct stemming from actions, intentions, and consequences. Over time, the concept of evil has evolved and been linked to various factors such as survival and self-preservation, social and cultural norms, as well as religious and spiritual beliefs.

Humans are inherently capable of both good and evil actions, influenced by a complex interplay of genetics, environment, upbringing, personal experiences, and cultural norms. Evil can be taught or learned through social conditioning, trauma, ideologies promoting hatred or violence, and a lack of empathy or moral guidance. In the book of Genesis, God created Adam and Eve, the first humans. They lived under one rule: not to eat from the Tree of Knowledge of Good and Evil. This abstinence was meant to preserve their innocence and prevent them from becoming aware of the darker aspects of the world.

CRITICAL THINKING AND COGNITIVE DEVELOPMENT FRAMEWORK (CTCDF)

$$CTCDF = (CT \times CD) + (RT \times RD) + (IT \times ID) + (ET \times ED) + (TT \times TD)$$

Where:
CTCDF = Critical Thinking and Cognitive Development Framework
CT = Critical Thinking (analysis, evaluation, reasoning)
CD = Cognitive Development (education, literacy, scientific methods)
RT = Rudimentary Thinking (myths, traditions, authorities, experiences)

RD = Religious and Dogmatic Beliefs (cognitive biases, superstitions)

IT = Influential Thinkers (Socrates, Plato, Aristotle, Buddha, Charvaka)

ID = Intellectual Curiosity (philosophical inquiry, skepticism)

ET = Evolution of Thinking (Enlightenment, scientific revolutions)

ED = Empirical Evidence (simplicity, reason, empiricism)

TT = Time and Change (neutral measure, progression)

TD = Teaching and Learning Evil (social conditioning, trauma, ideologies)

FRAMEWORK COMPONENTS

1. Critical Thinking (CT): Analysis, evaluation, reasoning.
2. Cognitive Development (CD): Education, literacy, scientific methods.
3. Rudimentary Thinking (RT): Myths, traditions, authorities, experiences.
4. Influential Thinkers (IT): Socrates, Plato, Aristotle, Buddha, Charvaka.
5. Intellectual Curiosity (ID): Philosophical inquiry, skepticism.
6. Evolution of Thinking (ET): Enlightenment, scientific revolutions.
7. Empirical Evidence (ED): Simplicity, reason, empiricism.
8. Time and Change (TT): Neutral measure, progression.
9. Teaching and Learning Evil (TD): Social conditioning, trauma, ideologies.
10. Religious and Dogmatic Beliefs (RD): Cognitive biases, superstitions.

FRAMEWORK APPLICATIONS

1. Critical Thinking Development: Encouraging analysis, evaluation, and reasoning.
2. Education and Literacy: Fostering cognitive development and critical thinking.
3. Philosophical Inquiry: Promoting intellectual curiosity and skepticism.
4. Scientific Methods and Empiricism: Emphasizing simplicity, reason, and evidence.
5. Social and Cultural Analysis: Understanding the evolution of thinking and beliefs.
6. Ethics and Morality: Examining the teaching and learning of evil.
7. Personal Growth and Development: Recognizing the impact of time and change.
8. Influential Thinkers and Ideas: Studying the contributions of notable individuals.

In the Bible, Satan is frequently depicted as a fallen angel, expelled from heaven for rebelling against God. Some interpretations suggest that God created Satan as a servant or angel, but Satan later rebelled and became corrupt. However, the concept of slavery does not align with the idea of a loving and just God. Many religious traditions emphasize God's desire for humanity's freedom and partnership, and in Christianity, God is often seen as a liberator, freeing people from sin, oppression, and bondage. Jesus' teachings emphasize love, compassion, and the inherent worth and dignity of all individuals. Some people see Satan as a symbolic representation of human sin and rebellion rather than a literal being, representing the collective shadow or darker aspects of human nature that emerged as humans developed and struggled with their own morality and free will.

THEOLOGICAL FRAMEWORK FOR UNDERSTANDING SATAN (TFUS)

$$TFUS = (BI \times SI) + (CI \times FI) + (TI \times HI) + (SI \times DI) + (RI \times LI)$$

Where:
   TFUS = Theological Framework for Understanding Satan
   BI = Biblical Interpretation (fallen angel, rebellion, expulsion)
   SI = Servant or Angel (created by God, later corrupted)
   CI = Conceptual Inconsistency (slavery, loving and just God)
   FI = Freedom and Partnership (God's desire, liberator, Jesus' teachings)
   TI = Theological Interpretation (symbolic representation, human sin, rebellion)
   HI = Human Nature (collective shadow, darker aspects, morality, free will)
   SI = Sin and Rebellion (human struggle, emergence of morality)
   DI = Duality of Human Nature (good and evil, light and dark)
   RI = Religious Traditions (emphasizing freedom, love, compassion)
   LI = Liberation and Redemption (God's role, Jesus' teachings)

FRAMEWORK COMPONENTS

1. Biblical Interpretation (BI): Fallen angel, rebellion, expulsion.
2. Servant or Angel (SI): Created by God, later corrupted.
3. Conceptual Inconsistency (CI): Slavery, loving and just God.
4. Theological Interpretation (TI): Symbolic representation, human sin, rebellion.
5. Human Nature (HI): Collective shadow, darker aspects, morality, free will.
6. Sin and Rebellion (SI): Human struggle, emergence of morality.
7. Duality of Human Nature (DI): Good and evil, light and dark.
8. Religious Traditions (RI): Emphasizing freedom, love, compassion.
9. Liberation and Redemption (LI): God's role, Jesus' teachings.
10. Freedom and Partnership (FI): God's desire, liberator, Jesus' teachings.

FRAMEWORK APPLICATIONS

1. Theological Discussion: Exploring the concept of Satan and its implications.
2. Biblical Analysis: Examining the depiction of Satan in scripture.
3. Philosophical Inquiry: Investigating the nature of good and evil.
4. Psychological Insight: Understanding the human struggle with morality.
5. Religious Education: Teaching the principles of freedom and partnership.
6. Personal Reflection: Contemplating the symbolism of Satan in one's life.
7. Ethical Considerations: Evaluating the impact of human sin and rebellion.
8. Spiritual Growth: Embracing the liberating power of God's love

TANGIBLE IDEAS ROOTED IN IMPRESSIONS

Over the course of my life, I have consistently exhibited a receptiveness to novel concepts and, eagerly embracing them at their initial introduction. However, as I dive deeper into these concepts, I uncover hidden aspects and truths that were not immediately apparent. Rather than becoming ensnared by superficial impressions, I prefer to focus on the approachable, allowing diverse thoughts to coalesce and form a more comprehensive understanding of the subject matter at hand.

IDEA EXPLORATION FRAMEWORK (IEF)

IEF = (RI x RD) + (NI x NA) + (DI x DA) + (CI x CA) + (TI x TA)

Where:
- IEF = Idea Exploration Framework
- RI = Receptive Introduction (novel concepts, eagerness)
- RD = Receptive Depth (hidden aspects, truths, exploration)
- NI = Nuanced Investigation (approachable, diverse thoughts)
- NA = Nuanced Awareness (comprehensive understanding, subject matter)
- DI = Diverse Insights (coalescing, forming, understanding)
- DA = Diverse Awareness (superficial, impressions, avoidance)
- CI = Comprehensive Insight (focus, clarity, subject matter)
- CA = Comprehensive Awareness (understanding, nuances, depth)
- TI = Tangible Ideas (rooted, impressions, exploration)
- TA = Tangible Awareness (approachable, diverse, comprehensive)

FRAMEWORK COMPONENTS
1. Receptive Introduction (RI): Novel concepts, eagerness, openness.
2. Nuanced Investigation (NI): Approachable, diverse thoughts, exploration.
3. Diverse Insights (DI): Coalescing, forming, understanding, nuances.
4. Comprehensive Insight (CI): Focus, clarity, subject matter, depth.
5. Tangible Ideas (TI): Rooted, impressions, exploration, approachable.
6. Receptive Depth (RD): Hidden aspects, truths, exploration, understanding.
7. Nuanced Awareness (NA): Comprehensive understanding, subject matter, nuances.
8. Diverse Awareness (DA): Superficial, impressions, avoidance, exploration.
9. Comprehensive Awareness (CA): Understanding, nuances, depth, clarity.
10. Tangible Awareness (TA): Approachable, diverse, comprehensive, exploration.

FRAMEWORK APPLICATIONS

1. Critical Thinking: Embracing receptive introduction and nuanced investigation.
2. Idea Generation: Fostering diverse insights and comprehensive awareness.
3. Problem-Solving: Applying tangible ideas and comprehensive insight.
4. Personal Growth: Cultivating receptive depth and nuanced awareness.
5. Philosophical Inquiry: Exploring diverse awareness and comprehensive understanding.
6. Creativity and Innovation: Encouraging approachable and tangible ideas.
7. Knowledge Acquisition: Pursuing nuanced investigation and diverse insights.
8. Wisdom Development: Embracing comprehensive awareness and tangible awareness.

Throughout my lifetime, I have actively avoided engaging with, endorsing, or promoting biblical literature. My strong conviction is that close-minded thinking and outdated viewpoints hinder personal growth and restrict individuals from reaching their full potential.

The concept of compression within religious texts requires a deep understanding of the material in order to grasp its true significance. Despite appearing to be a condensed version, the true essence lies within the content.

In texts such as the Bible and Quran where punishment is frequently mentioned, what does the act of sacrifice truly represent if the outcome is already predetermined and unfavorable for all?

Using these teachings as a means of control can have adverse effects on progress and can even lead to destruction, as evidenced by wars and conflicts. Discrimination and resistance serve no real purpose, so why do we continue to justify them?

The conflicts that have arisen include the Crusades, Wars of Religion, Islamic Conquests, Reformation Wars, Hindu-Muslim Wars, Buddhist Wars, Jewish Wars, Sikh Wars, Taiping Rebellion, and Nigerian Civil War. In more recent times, there have been significant disputes rooted in religious differences such as the Syrian Civil War (2011-present), Iraq War (2003-2011), Israeli-Palestinian Conflict (1948-present), Kashmir Conflict

(1947-present), and Yemeni Civil War (2015-present). The period between 1450-1750 saw witch hunts and trials resulting in around 40,000-60,000 executions primarily targeting women. The Crusades from 1095-1291 claimed an estimated 1-3 million lives and the Inquisition from 1184-1834 led to an estimated 150,000-300,000 executions. The Thirty Years War (1618-1648) resulted in an estimated 8-12 million deaths while the Taiping Rebellion (1850-1864) caused approximately 20-30 million deaths. More recently, terrorist acts such as the devastating 9/11 attacks in 2001 resulting in 2,996 deaths and the reign of ISIS from 2014 to 2019 causing an estimated 20,000-30,000 deaths have been linked to religious conflicts. Sectarian violence has also been observed during India's Partition in 1947 with a death toll of approximately 1-2 million and ongoing conflicts in Nigeria have resulted in an estimated death toll of 10,000-20,000 due to Boko Haram. Other notable conflicts include Lebanon from 1975 to1990 with a death toll of around 120,000-150,000 and Sri Lanka from 1983 to2009 claiming approximately 80,000-100,000 lives. When the total number of lives lost due to religious strife is considered, one may question the state of humanity and the values of compassion and peaceful coexistence.

RELIGIOUS CONFLICT FRAMEWORK (RCF)

$$RCF = (RI \times RD) + (CT \times CD) + (PR \times PD) + (VR \times VD) + (HR \times HD)$$

Where:
RCF = Religious Conflict Framework
RI = Religious Ideology (close-minded thinking, outdated viewpoints)
RD = Restricted Development (personal growth, full potential)
CT = Compression and Truth (deep understanding, true significance)
CD = Condensed and Distorted (punishment, predetermined outcome)
PR = Promotion and Control (adverse effects, progress, destruction)
PD = Punishment and Discrimination (wars, conflicts, resistance)
VR = Violence and Resistance (justification, conflicts, wars)
VD = Violence and Destruction (history, death toll, suffering)
HR = Humanitarian and Rational (compassion, peaceful coexistence, values)
HD = Humanitarian and Diplomatic (resolution, understanding, peace)

FRAMEWORK COMPONENTS
 1. Religious Ideology (RI): Close-minded thinking, outdated viewpoints.
 2. Compression and Truth (CT): Deep understanding, true significance.
 3. Promotion and Control (PR): Adverse effects, progress, destruction.
 4. Violence and Resistance (VR): Justification, conflicts, wars.
 5. Humanitarian and Rational (HR): Compassion, peaceful coexistence, values.
 6. Restricted Development (RD): Personal growth, full potential.
 7. Condensed and Distorted (CD): Punishment, predetermined outcome.
 8. Punishment and Discrimination (PD): Wars, conflicts, resistance.
 9. Violence and Destruction (VD): History, death toll, suffering.
10. Humanitarian and Diplomatic (HD): Resolution, understanding, peace.

FRAMEWORK APPLICATIONS
 1. Conflict Resolution: Encouraging humanitarian and diplomatic approaches.
 2. Personal Growth: Fostering open-minded thinking and development.
 3. Social Commentary: Analyzing religious ideology and its impact.
 4. Historical Reflection: Understanding the consequences of religious conflicts.
 5. Peacebuilding: Promoting compassion, peaceful coexistence, and values.
 6. Critical Thinking: Examining compression, truth, and promotion.
 7. Human Rights: Addressing punishment, discrimination, and violence.
 8. Philosophical Inquiry: Exploring the nature of religious conflicts and resolution.

In a society shaped by societal norms, preconceived notions, and financial influence, it is natural to question the necessity of challenging the established order. However, the status quo was designed to facilitate progress and development. Without change, there would be no room for growth, and stagnation would prevail.

In my solitude, while others may engage in various activities to occupy their time, I find solace in the realm of thought. My mind wanders freely, pondering both the profound and the mundane, delving into the depths of contemplation.

CONTEMPLATIVE FRAMEWORK (CF)

CF = (SQ x SR) + (PN x PC) + (FI x FR) + (CT x CR) + (MD x MR)

Where:
CF = Contemplative Framework
SQ = Status Quo (established order, norms)
SR = Status Quo Reevaluation (necessity, challenge)
PN = Preconceived Notions (societal expectations, influence)
PC = Progressive Change (growth, development, progress)
FI = Financial Influence (power dynamics, interests)
FR = Financial Reformation (equity, accessibility, justice)
CT = Contemplative Thinking (solitude, reflection, insight)
CR = Critical Reflection (analysis, evaluation, wisdom)
MD = Mindful Deliberation (pondering, contemplation, depth)
MR = Meaningful Realization (understanding, awareness, growth)

FRAMEWORK COMPONENTS
1. Status Quo (SQ): Established order, norms, expectations.
2. Preconceived Notions (PN): Societal expectations, influence, bias.
3. Financial Influence (FI): Power dynamics, interests, inequality.
4. Contemplative Thinking (CT): Solitude, reflection, insight.
5. Mindful Deliberation (MD): Pondering, contemplation, depth.
6. Status Quo Reevaluation (SR): Necessity, challenge, reflection.
7. Progressive Change (PC): Growth, development, progress.
8. Financial Reformation (FR): Equity, accessibility, justice.
9. Critical Reflection (CR): Analysis, evaluation, wisdom.
10. Meaningful Realization (MR): Understanding, awareness, growth.

FRAMEWORK APPLICATIONS
1. Personal Growth: Embracing contemplative thinking and mindful deliberation.
2. Critical Thinking: Challenging preconceived notions and financial influence.
3. Philosophical Inquiry: Exploring the nature of reality and human existence.
4. Creative Expression: Finding inspiration in solitude and contemplation.

5. Leadership and Innovation: Encouraging progressive change and financial reformation.
6. Mental Health and Wellness: Cultivating mindful deliberation and meaningful realization.
7. Social Commentary: Analyzing the impact of societal norms and financial influence.
8. piritual Exploration: Delving into the depths of contemplation and critical reflection.

Wave formations, understanding the cyclical rhythm of nature, compression, and energy build up. When you understand the basic principles of chaos, you understand the basic principles of nature.The basic principles of all things, and how they come together and form. It's usually due to some underlying current, a wave forming. Created by friction beneath the surface.This is where your storms emerge, the hurricanes, earthquakes and tornadoes. The wild and rapid raging fires. Earthquakes release seismic energy, hurricanes and tornadoes are fueled by thermal energy, and tsunamis are triggered by the release of gravitational energy. Everybody knows fire needs energy to ignite and sustain itself. The wind just influences its behavior.

In wave interference, also known as meddling, tampering with, and trespassing, compression causes a build-up of energy. When I hold something in for an extended period of time, the energy accumulates, and the outcome upon release is unpredictable. (I attempt to modify the wave's course, altering its magnitude, amplitude, and direction, essentially changing the wave's latitude and longitude.)

When two waves interact, their behavior depends on their phase, amplitude, and direction. Identical waves that are out of phase can cancel each other out, resulting in a diminished or flat wave. Conversely, waves in phase (where crests meet crests and troughs meet troughs) can reinforce each other, creating a larger wave. Waves meeting at an angle can change direction, forming a new wave pattern. When waves encounter an obstacle or a narrow opening, they can bend around it, creating a distinct wave pattern.

Earthquakes can cause tsunamis, displacement generates waves. Earthquakes can't directly trigger tornadoes, but they can trigger landslides or soil liquefaction, altering wind patterns contributing to the formation of a tornado.

Hurricanes form over warm ocean waters due to a combination of atmospheric and oceanic conditions, like low pressure, high humidity, and elevated sea surface temperatures. If an earthquake triggers a significant landslide or sediment disturbance in a coastal region, it could potentially disrupt the local currents and temperature. The disruption could influence the formation or trajectory of a hurricane.

Despite the potential inaccuracies of weather forecasts, observing patterns, formations, and paths can provide valuable insights.

WAVE DYNAMICS FRAMEWORK (WDF)

WDF = (WF x WC) + (CE x CU) + (EI x EU) + (TI x TU) + (WI x WU)

Where:
WDF = Wave Dynamics Framework
WF = Wave Formation (cyclical rhythm, compression, energy build-up)
WC = Wave Compression (friction, underlying current, wave interference)
CE = Chaotic Energy (seismic, thermal, gravitational, release)
CU = Chaotic Unpredictability (storms, earthquakes, hurricanes, wildfires)
EI = Energy Interference (phase, amplitude, direction, interaction)
EU = Energy Union (reinforcement, cancellation, wave pattern)
TI = Triggering Events (earthquakes, landslides, soil liquefaction, tornadoes)
TU = Tsunami Unleashing (displacement, waves, oceanic conditions)
WI = Weather Insights (patterns, formations, paths, forecasts)
WU = Weather Uncertainty (inaccuracies, observations, chaos)

FRAMEWORK COMPONENTS
1. Wave Formation (WF): Cyclical rhythm, compression, energy build-up.
2. Chaotic Energy:(CE): Seismic, thermal, gravitational, release.
3. Energy Interference (EI): Phase, amplitude, direction, interaction.

4. Triggering Events (TI): Earthquakes, landslides, soil liquefaction, tornadoes.
5. Weather Insights (WI): Patterns, formations, paths, forecasts.
6. Wave Compression (WC): Friction, underlying current, wave interference.
7. Chaotic Unpredictability (CU): Storms, earthquakes, hurricanes, wildfires.
8. Energy Union (EU): Reinforcement, cancellation, wave pattern.
9. Tsunami Unleashing (TU): Displacement, waves, oceanic conditions.
10. Weather Uncertainty (WU): Inaccuracies, observations, chaos.

FRAMEWORK APPLICATIONS

1. Natural Disaster Analysis: Understanding wave dynamics and chaotic energy.
2. Weather Forecasting: Observing patterns, formations, and paths.
3. Earth Science Research: Studying wave formation, compression, and interference.
4. Environmental Monitoring: Tracking triggering events and tsunami unleashing.
5. Chaos Theory Exploration: Delving into chaotic unpredictability and energy union.
6. Climate Modeling: Accounting for weather uncertainty and wave dynamics.
7. Geological Hazard Assessment: Evaluating earthquake and landslide risks.
8. Oceanographic Studies: Investigating oceanic conditions and wave patterns.

ενθάρρυνση προσδέματος / LIGAND ENCOURAGEMENT
מרכיבים בנמלים אחרים / INGREDIENTS IN OTHER PORTS

In my pursuit of introspection, I embarked on a journey of self-discovery that led me to explore the depths of my inner darkness, devoid of conventional limitations. I sought to comprehend the intense emotions that required control, needed to remain hidden, and tucked away. Nestled, but the emotions wouldn't settle. I was lost in an unfamiliar place. Somewhere between here, there, and nowhere. The unfamiliar and unsettling became a haunting aspect of my reality leaving me studying e-motion.

E-motion, embodying energy in motion, subject to interference due to various factors and patterns. This interference generates static, which accumulates in large quantities, analogous to dark matter. Emotion acts as a driving force, influencing all phenomena and interactions. At the molecular level, ligands, characterized as electron donors capable of binding to receptors, play a pivotal role in facilitating chemical reactions and signaling processes. Mechanical energy, associated with the motion of objects, and stored energy, encompassing potential and elastic energy, manifest as forms of motion.

In my exploration of emotion, interference emerged as an unavoidable occurrence, akin to the resonance generated by plucked strings. This catalytic effect initiated a cascading sequence of events, reminiscent of the proverbial butterfly effect. On a cosmic scale, dark matter exerted its gravitational influence, while electromagnetic forces assumed a dominant role.

At its core, energy can be traced back to emotions or energy in motion. This fundamental aspect of energy as emotion permeates the universe, shaping its dynamics and driving its progression. From the tiniest particles to the farthest corners of space, the universe's dynamics and evolution are profoundly influenced by the inherent nature of e-motion.

EMOTIONAL DYNAMICS FRAMEWORK (EDF)

$$EDF = (EI \times EM) + (IF \times IS) + (LF \times LR) + (ME \times MS) + (DE \times DU)$$

Where:
EDF = Emotional Dynamics Framework
EI = Emotional Introspection (self-discovery, inner darkness)
EM = Emotional Motion (energy in motion, e-motion)
IF = Interference and Friction (static, accumulation,
      dark matter)
IS = Influencing Forces (emotional driving force, phenomena,
      interactions)
LF = Ligand Functions (electron donors, receptors, chemical
      reactions)
LR = Ligand Receptors (signaling processes, molecular level)
ME = Mechanical Energy (motion, objects, stored energy)

MS = Molecular Signaling (chemical reactions,
      energy transfer)
DE = Dark Energy (cosmic scale, gravitational influence)
DU = Dynamic Universe (evolution, progression, emotional
      dynamics)

FRAMEWORK COMPONENTS
1. Emotional Introspection (EI): Self-discovery, inner darkness.
2. Emotional Motion (EM): Energy in motion, e-motion.
3. Interference and Friction (IF): Static, accumulation, dark matter.
4. Ligand Functions (LF): Electron donors, receptors, chemical reactions.
5. Mechanical Energy (ME): Motion, objects, stored energy.
6. Influencing Forces (IS): Emotional driving force, phenomena, interactions.
7. Ligand Receptors (LR): Signaling processes, molecular level.
8. Molecular Signaling (MS): Chemical reactions, energy transfer.
9. Dark Energy (DE): Cosmic scale, gravitational influence.
10. Dynamic Universe (DU): Evolution, progression, emotional dynamics.

FRAMEWORK APPLICATIONS
1. Personal Growth: Exploring emotional introspection and emotional motion.
2. Physics and Chemistry: Understanding ligand functions and molecular signaling.
3. Cosmology: Examining dark energy and the dynamic universe.
4. Psychology and Neuroscience: Investigating influencing forces and interference.
5. Philosophy and Spirituality: Contemplating the nature of emotional dynamics.
6. Energy and Motion: Analyzing mechanical energy and stored energy.
7. Emotional Intelligence: Developing self-awareness and emotional regulation.
8. Complex Systems: Studying the butterfly effect and cascading sequences.

Have you ever encountered someone attempting to sell you an idea, only to find that the concept itself was just as flawed as the application being developed? It's like claiming that millions of people love a particular program, but the company behind it has hired workers specializing in app marketing rather than focusing on the quality of the application. These companies often possess a sophisticated ASO (App Store Optimization) algorithm designed to enhance an application's visibility and ranking on various platforms. The role of these workers is to act as genuine users, utilizing networks to ensure the uploaded false data appears authentic and accurate.

Each day, I embark on a journey of ideation, where I craft frameworks, lay foundations, and chart paths forward. While I might not possess formal education in every field I delve into, conceptual thinking, like anything involving reasoning, has its advantages and disadvantages.

IDEATION AND INNOVATION FRAMEWORK (IIF)

IIF = (CI x CD) + (ASO x AD) + (FF x FD) + (CT x CA) + (PN x PD)

Where:
IIF = Ideation and Innovation Framework
CI = Conceptual Ideation (idea generation, flaws, application)
CD = Critical Development (quality, focus, marketing)
ASO = App Store Optimization (algorithm, visibility, ranking)
AD = Artificial Data (false, authenticity, accuracy)
FF = Foundational Frameworks (conceptual thinking, reasoning)
FD = Field Development (education, advantages, disadvantages)
CT = Creative Thinking (journey, ideation, innovation)
CA = Critical Analysis (evaluation, improvement)
PN = Path Navigation (charting, forward thinking)
PD = Progressive Development (growth, iteration)

FRAMEWORK COMPONENTS
1. Conceptual Ideation (CI): Idea generation, flaws, application.
2. App Store Optimization (ASO): Algorithm, visibility, ranking.
3. Foundational Frameworks (FF): Conceptual thinking, reasoning.
4. Creative Thinking (CT): Journey, ideation, innovation.
5. Critical Development (CD): Quality, focus, marketing.
6. Artificial Data (AD): False, authenticity, accuracy.
7. Field Development (FD): Education, advantages, disadvantages.

8. Critical Analysis (CA): Evaluation, improvement.
9. Path Navigation (PN): Charting, forward thinking.
10. Progressive Development (PD): Growth, iteration.

FRAMEWORK APPLICATIONS

1. Idea Generation: Embracing conceptual ideation and creative thinking.
2. App Development: Focusing on quality and critical development.
3. Marketing Strategy: Avoiding artificial data and emphasizing authenticity.
4. Personal Growth: Navigating paths forward and embracing progressive development.
5. Innovation and Entrepreneurship: Leveraging foundational frameworks and critical analysis.
6. Education and Learning: Recognizing the advantages and disadvantages of field development.
7. Critical Thinking and Reasoning: Developing skills in conceptual thinking and evaluation.

In a one-sided world (unilateral) devoid of utilitarian principles, a hypothetical concept emerges - a world guided by a theory that prioritizes maximizing overall happiness, well-being, and utility for the majority of people. However, such a world, lacking symmetry and reciprocity, would inevitably cause suffering for some individuals. The asymmetry, where the benefits are not equally distributed, highlights the limitations of one-sided thinking.

The concept of left and right-sided thinking, often referred to as the left and right wing, introduces the idea of a "right" and "wrong" way of thinking based on conceptual frameworks. The dichotomy can be traced back to the French Revolution, where those who sat on the left side of the National Assembly were generally more liberal, while those on the right were more conservative. Over time, these terms have come to represent a broader spectrum of political ideologies, with the left typically associated with progressive values such as social justice and egalitarianism, and the right with more traditional values such as patriotism and free markets.

In the political landscape, the left and right are often viewed as polar opposites. However, it's crucial to recognize that these ideologies are not mutually exclusive. The dynamic between the left and right is often characterized by tension and conflict. This is because they frequently have contrasting visions for society. Despite their differences, both the left and the right play a vital role in a healthy democracy. They represent distinct perspectives on significant issues, and their competition ensures that all voices are represented. Without the left, society might become stagnant and oppressive. Alternatively, without the right, society might become chaotic and unstable.

In a vibrant political system, it's crucial to recognize that the left and right are intertwined and necessary components. Their interactions, although often contentious, facilitate a balanced and inclusive society. As I delved into the intricacies of different ethical viewpoints, a unique concept emerged: Unilateral Utilitarianism (UU). UU merges the principles of unilateral decision-making with a utilitarian objective. It establishes a framework that balances the necessity for prompt, unilateral action with the ethical imperative of maximizing overall well-being.

EXPLORING THE FUNDAMENTALS OF UNILATERAL UTILITARIANISM: CORE PRINCIPLES, HISTORICAL CONTEXT, AND KEY CONCEPTS

Maximize overall happiness. Prioritize actions that maximize overall happiness and well-being.	Universal Consideration: Consider the happiness and well-being of all individuals, without exception.	Unilateral decision-making: Make decisions based on UU principles, even if others do not reciprocate.	Long-term thinking: Prioritize long-term happiness and well-being over short-term gains.	Happiness metrics: Use data and metrics to measure happiness and inform decision-making.
Stakeholder engagement: Engage with stakeholders to understand their happiness and well-being needs.	Transparency and accountability: Openly share UU metrics and progress, ensuring accountability.	Continuous improvement: Regularly refine and adapt UU strategies based on data insights.	Moral absolutism: Apply UU principles consistently, without exception or compromise.	Empathy and compassion: Prioritize empathy and compassion in decision-making processes.

By following these principles, individuals and organizations can effectively apply Unilateral Utilitarianism, prioritizing happiness and well-being in decision-making processes.

Mission: To foster a global community that advances happiness and well-being through the principles of Unilateral Utilitarianism.

HISTORY

Classical Utilitarianism: UU draws from classical utilitarianism, which emerged in the 18th century.

Jeremy Bentham: Bentham's work on pleasure and pain laid the groundwork for utilitarian thought.

John Stuart Mill: Mill's refinements on Bentham's ideas further developed utilitarian philosophy.

MODERN DEVELOPMENTS: CONTEMPORARY THINKERS HAVE EXPANDED AND ADAPTED UTILITARIANISM, LEADING TO UU.

Key Concepts:

Happiness: The primary goal of UU, encompassing pleasure, satisfaction, and well-being.

Utility: The measure of happiness or well-being generated by an action or decision.

Consequentialism: The idea that moral judgments should be based on the consequences of actions.

Moral absolutism: UU's commitment to applying its principles consistently, without exception.

Empathy and compassion: Essential components of UU, ensuring consideration for all individuals' happiness.

Rational decision-making: UU's emphasis on informed, data-driven decision-making.

Categories:
- UU Fundamentals:_ Introduction to UU principles, history, and key concepts.
- Happiness and Well-being:_ Research and articles on happiness, well-being, and quality of life.
- Decision-Making and Ethics:_ Resources on UU-based decision-making, ethics, and moral philosophy.
- Economics and Policy:_ Applications of UU in economics, policy-making, and governance.
- Social Justice and Equality:_ UU perspectives on social justice, equality, and human rights.
- Environmental Sustainability:_ UU approaches to environmental sustainability and climate change.
- Health and Healthcare:_ UU applications in healthcare, public health, and health policy.
- Education and Personal Development:_ UU-based resources for education and personal growth.

Although creating an app is accessible to many individuals, the question arises: Who genuinely desires to spend their days playing games?

Legislative Approach	Executive Approach	Judicial Approach	Public Engagement
Introduce UU-based legislation: Propose laws and policies that align with UU principles, prioritizing overall happiness and well-being.	Issue executive orders that align with UU principles, prioritizing happiness and well-being.	Apply UU principles in judicial decisions, considering the potential happiness impact of rulings.	Educate citizens about UU: Raise awareness about UU principles and their application in politics.

Establish a UU Oversight Committee: Create a committee to review and ensure that policies align with UU principles.	Apply UU principles in decision-making processes, considering the potential happiness impact of actions	Set precedents for UU-based decisions, guiding future judicial decisions.	Encourage public participation: Engage citizens in the decision-making process, ensuring their voices are heard.
Conduct Happiness Impact Assessments (HIAs): Require HIAs for proposed policies to evaluate their potential impact on happiness.	Appoint advisors knowledgeable in UU to inform decision-making.	Use the UU framework to guide decision-making, considering the potential happiness impact of choices.	Develop policies that promote flexible work arrangements or wellness programs. Promote a culture that values happiness and well-being.
Consult with experts in UU to inform policy decisions.	Incorporate UU principles into the company's mission, vision, and values.	By taking a comprehensive political approach, governments can effectively implement Unilateral Utilitarianism, prioritizing the happiness and well-being of citizens.	Develop and track metrics that measure employee satisfaction and customer well-being.

By integrating UU into business operations, companies can prioritize happiness and well-being, leading to increased employee satisfaction, customer loyalty, and long-term success.

POTENTIAL METRICS AND DATA POINTS: MEASURING THE EFFECTIVENESS OF UNILATERAL UTILITARIANISM IN VARIOUS CONTEXTS:

Happiness Metrics:	Business Metrics:	Social Justice Metrics:	Data Points :	Data-driven insights en-
Self-reported happiness levels (e.g., surveys, questionnaires)	Employee engagement and satisfaction	Reduction in inequality metrics (e.g., income, education, healthcare)	Demographic data (e.g., age, gender, income, education)	able informed decisions that maximize happiness and well-being.
Emotional well-being indices (e.g., anxiety, stress, life satisfaction)	Customer satisfaction and loyalty	Increase in social mobility metrics	Behavioral data (e.g., habits, preferences, values)	Data tracks progress, identifying areas for improvement and optimizing UU strategies.
Psychological well-being metrics (e.g., flourishing, resilience)	Revenue growth and profitability	Improvement in marginalized group outcomes (e.g., employment, housing, education)	Outcome data (e.g., health, education, employment)	Transparent metrics and data foster trust and collaboration among stakeholders.
Physical health indicators (e.g., blood pressure, BMI, sleep quality)	Social responsibility and reputation metrics	Social responsibility and reputation metrics	Feedback and sentiment analysis data	Data enables comparison and benchmarking, facilitating knowledge sharing and best practices.

By leveraging metrics and data, UU implementation becomes more effective, efficient, and impactful, ultimately leading to increased happiness and well-being.

POTENTIAL CAPABILITIES FOR AN ORGANIZATION OR INDIVIDUAL IMPLEMENTING UNILATERAL UTILITARIANISM

Decision-Making Capabilities	Data and Analytics Capabilities	Strategic Planning Capabilities:	Communication and Engagement Capabilities:	Change Management Capabilities: UU cultural integration
Happiness impact assessment	Data collection and management	UU-aligned goal setting	UU education and training	Employee engagement and development
Decision analysis and evaluation	Happiness metrics development and tracking	Strategic planning and implementation	Stakeholder engagement and communication	Continuous improvement and adaptation
Stakeholder engagement and consideration	Data-driven decision-making	Continuous monitoring and evaluation	Feedback mechanisms and sentiment analysis. Transparency and reporting	Cross-sector collaboration Collective impact initiatives

HAPPINESS METRICS FRAMEWORK

Subjective Well-being (SWB): Measure individuals' self-reported happiness, life satisfaction, and emotional well-being.

Psychological Well-being (PWB): Assess psychological functioning, including autonomy, competence, and relatedness.

Physical Well-being (PhWB): Evaluate physical health, comfort, and functioning.

Social Well-being (SoWB): Examine social connections, relationships, and community engagement.

Environmental Well-being (EnWB): Assess access to natural environments, environmental quality, and sustainability.

METRICS AND INDICATORS

Happiness Score: A composite score based on SWB, PWB, PhWB, SoWB, and EnWB.

Life Satisfaction: Self-reported satisfaction with life, using scales like Cantril's Ladder.

Emotional Experience: Frequency and intensity of positive/negative emotions.

Psychological Functioning: Scales like Ryff's Psychological Well-being or Diener's Flourishing Scale.

Physical Health: Self-reported health, chronic conditions, and health behaviors.

Social Connections: Strength and quality of relationships, social support, and community engagement.

Environmental Quality: Access to green spaces, air/water quality, and environmental concerns.

DATA COLLECTION METHODS

Surveys: Online or offline questionnaires, like the Oxford Happiness Questionnaire.

Interviews: In-depth, semi-structured interviews to gather qualitative insights.

Observational Studies: Longitudinal or cross-sectional studies observing behavior and outcomes.

Administrative Data: Utilize existing data from organizations, governments, or social media.

DATA ANALYSIS AND INTERPRETATION

Descriptive Statistics: Summarize and visualize data using means, medians, and distributions.

Inferential Statistics: Use regression, ANOVA, or machine learning to identify relationships and predict outcomes.

Benchmarking: Compare happiness scores across groups, organizations, or regions.

Trend Analysis: Monitor changes in happiness metrics over time. (Happiness metrics framework) effectively measure and evaluate happiness impacts, identify areas for improvement, and inform data-driven decisions.

While developing frameworks and applications may seem straightforward, the real challenge lies in their implementation.

Q1. What is the main purpose of the UU Decision Maker app?
1. To maximize happiness and streamline decision-making
2. To track user fitness activities
3. To manage personal finances
4. To create social media content

Q2. Which feature of the UU Decision Maker app helps in engaging with stakeholders and sharing insights?
1. Collaboration platform
2. Data analytics
3. Decision-making toolkit
4. Accountability mechanisms

Q3. Which platform is NOT mentioned as supported by the UU Decision Maker app?
1. Smartwatch app
2. Web app
3. Mobile app
4. API integration

Q4. What should users do after choosing the optimal option in the UU Decision Maker app?
1. Monitor and adjust
2. Delete the data
3. Start a new decision process
4. Consult an expert

Q5. Who is NOT listed as a target audience for the UU Decision Maker app?
1. School students
2. Business leaders
3. Policy makers
4. Individuals

Q6. What does the 'data analytics' feature of the UU Decision Maker app provide?
1. Leverages data to inform decisions and measure outcomes
2. Tracks users' daily steps
3. Analyzes financial investments
4. Organizes calendar events

Q7. Which feature of the UU Decision Maker app enhances transparency and accountability?
1. Accountability mechanisms
2. Collaboration platform
3. Customizable frameworks
4. Decision-making toolkit

Q8. What is the first step in the decision-making process using the UU Decision Maker app?
1. Define objectives
2. Evaluate options
3. Choose the optimal option
4. Gather insights

Q9. What does the UU in UU Decision Maker stand for?
1. Unilateral Utilitarianism
2. Universal Utility
3. Ultimate Understanding
4. Unified Usage

Q10. Which tool in the UU Decision Maker app helps to assess potential courses of action and their consequences?
1. Evaluate options
2. Define objectives
3. Monitor and adjust
4. Choose the optimal option

The execution of an action can simultaneously contribute to both the origin and resolution of a problem. Following basic instructions, such as looking both ways before crossing the road, is often overlooked by individuals. This raises the question of assigning responsibility in the event of an accident involving a driver and a pedestrian. Typically, each party blames the other, but who has the legal right of way? Does a pedestrian have priority when the traffic light is green, even if they are not using a designated crosswalk? What happens if a driver fails to notice a pedestrian emerging from between parked vehicles? This is where critical thinking becomes essential. By breaking down the situation and examining all relevant factors, a clearer understanding of the incident can be achieved.

An actual equation based on the Responsibility Assignment Formula (RAF):

$$RAF = (0.3P + 0.2F) + (0.2D + 0.1A) + (0.1C + 0.05S) + (0.05T + 0.05L)$$

Where:
P = Pedestrian's adherence to traffic rules (0-1)
F = Pedestrian's visibility and awareness (0-1)
D = Driver's attention and caution (0-1)
A = Driver's adherence to traffic rules (0-1)
C = Contributing circumstances (weather, road conditions, etc.) (0-1)
S = Severity of the accident (0-1)
T = Traffic light/control indicator (0-1)
L = Location and designation of crosswalk (0-1)

This equation assigns weights to each factor, allowing for a numerical calculation of responsibility. The weights can be adjusted based on specific legal frameworks and circumstances.

Example:
  P = 0.8 (pedestrian followed traffic rules)
  F = 0.9 (pedestrian was visible and aware)
  D = 0.6 (driver was somewhat attentive)
  A = 0.7 (driver mostly followed traffic rules)
  C = 0.4 (weather and road conditions contributed somewhat)
  S = 0.8 (severity of the accident was moderate)
  T = 0.9 (traffic light was in pedestrian's favor)
  L = 0.8 (pedestrian used a designated crosswalk)

  RAF = (0.3(0.8) + 0.2(0.9)) + (0.2(0.6) + 0.1(0.7)) + (0.1(0.4) + 0.05(0.8))
        + (0.05(0.9) + 0.05(0.8))
  RAF ≈ 3.43

In this example, the pedestrian bears approximately 34.3% of the responsibility, while the driver bears approximately 65.7%.

In a realm where existence, concepts, ideas, individuals, locations, and objects intertwine seamlessly with time and the human mind, an intricate web of interconnectedness is woven. Within this tapestry, emotions ebb and flow like waves of frequency, consuming energy and culminating in moments of frustration. Determining the optimal duration for engaging with an idea is a matter of debate, but I propose a limit of three hours. Beyond this point, comprehension wanes, and possession of knowledge loses its significance for me.

OPTIMAL ENGAGEMENT DURATION (OED) FORMULA

$$OED = (F \times I \times A) / (C \times R)$$

  Where:
      F = Focus (ability to concentrate)
      I = Intensity (level of mental engagement)
      A = Attention (available mental resources)
      C = Comprehension (threshold for absorbing information)
      R = Retention (ability to recall and apply knowledge)

PERSONALIZED ADJUSTMENT

To adapt this formula to individual needs, you can adjust the variables based on your learning style, attention span, and goals:

$$OED = (F \times I \times A) / (C \times R) \times (P \times L)$$

Where:
P = Personalized factor (adjusting for individual differences)
L = Learning style factor (accounting for unique learning approaches)

(My pursuit lies not in commercial transactions but in grasping the essence and depth of concepts.) To comprehend the intricate puzzle, I require all the fragments, fractions, pieces, parts, and compartments. Each element is vital to unraveling the concept's fragmented thinking.

Fragmented thinking is a cognitive process that involves breaking down complex problems or situations into smaller, more manageable components. This approach can be useful for understanding intricate concepts and making decisions. In quantum mechanics, fragmented thinking is essential for comprehending the wave-particle duality of matter and the superposition principle. By breaking down complex quantum systems into smaller, more manageable parts, it's easier to understand their behavior.

One of the fundamental concepts in thermodynamics is the fluctuation-dissipation theorem, which relates the fluctuations of a system to its dissipation of energy. This theorem has applications in a wide range of fields, including statistical mechanics, condensed matter physics, and biology.

How does an airplane achieve flight without a lift? Aerodynamic forces acting on the wings of an airplane generate lift. The pressure difference between the wing's upper and lower surfaces produces these forces. Factors such as the wing's shape, angle of attack, and the plane's speed influence the amount of lift generated. When faced with an upsetting situation, how do you respond: do you plot, scheme, plan, attack, or reflect? (How does propulsion manifest during combustion?) High pressure and high-velocity gases are produced through an explosive energy release.

This gas results from a rapid chemical reaction between fuel and oxidizer, leading to a significant increase in temperature and pressure.

Fragmented thinking, quantum mechanics, and thermodynamics are all interconnected disciplines that provide powerful tools for understanding the world around us, and ourselves.

FRAGMENTED THINKING FRAMEWORK (FTF)

Unravel complex concepts into manageable components

FTF Formula

$$FTF = (DC \times CC) + (ST \times RT) + (QT \times TT)$$

Where:
DC = Decomposition Complexity (breaking down complex problems)
CC = Component Connectivity (analyzing relationships between parts)
ST = Systems Thinking (considering the larger context)
RT = Reductionism Threshold (balancing detail and abstraction)
QT = Quantum Insight (applying wave-particle duality and superposition)
TT = Thermodynamic Efficiency (optimizing energy and resource allocation)

APPLICATIONS
1. Problem-solving: Break down complex issues into manageable parts.
2. Decision-making: Analyze component interactions and optimize outcomes.
3. Innovation: Apply quantum and thermodynamic principles to novel solutions.
4. Personal growth: Reflect on fragmented thinking to enhance self-awareness.

SELLABLE FRAMEWORK PACKAGES
1. Basic: FTF Fundamentals ($99) - E-book and webinar series.
2. Premium: FTF Pro ($299) - Personalized coaching and case studies.
3. Enterprise: FTF Team ($999) - Customized workshops and strategic planning.

FORMULA-BASED TOOLS
1. FTF Calculator: Software for calculating FTF scores.
2. FTF Simulator: Virtual lab for testing fragmented thinking scenarios.
3. FTF Analytics: Data-driven insights for optimizing complex systems.

CONSULTING SERVICES
1. Fragmented Thinking Assessment: Identify areas for improvement.
2. Customized FTF Strategy: Develop tailored solutions.
3. FTF Coaching: Guided practice for individuals and teams.

CERTIFICATION PROGRAMS
1. FTF Practitioner: Basic certification.
2. FTF Specialist: Advanced certification.
3. FTF Master: Expert-level certification.

BOOKS AND COURSES
1. "Mastering Fragmented Thinking" (book)
2. "FTF Fundamentals" (online course)
3. "Advanced FTF Applications" (workshop)

COMMUNITY AND SUPPORT
1. FTF Forum (online community)
2. FTF Newsletter (monthly updates)
3. FTF Webinars (regular expert sessions)

Within the realm of shared connections and ancestral telepathy, individuals possess the ability to tap into the collective consciousness, thereby accessing a repository of knowledge and wisdom. (土挖煤/digging coal from soil)

Upon occasion, I embark upon a journey, extracting coal from the depths of the earth. Propelled by the inherent challenge, transported to a realm of simplicity devoid of stark contrasts, where a profound connection emerges. However, establishing this connection necessitates substantial excavation, which presents potential risks, such as structural instability, gas accumulation, and environmental hazards.

(負じゃう 品ぐわ/it's negative.)

Through various processes involving friction, chemical reactions, electrical resistance, and nuclear reactions, energy can be generated. Coal, a fossil fuel, possesses stored energy that is released when subjected to combustion.

Combustion entails the release of heat and light, converting the chemical energy stored within coal into thermal energy. This thermal energy can be harnessed for power generation, enabling us to utilize the energy originally contained within coal.

Thermal energy represents the total internal energy of a system attributable to the motion of its constituent particles, such as atoms and molecules. It serves as an indicator of the system's temperature. The transfer of thermal energy from one system to another occurs due to temperature differences. (并妈无脑黑骨里砸温度怕/I'm not afraid of the temperature.)

I am familiar with the concept of temperature, the negative, and the experience of sitting in darkness. Heat naturally flows from systems with higher temperatures to those with lower temperatures. Electromagnetic radiation visible to the human eye exists within a specific range of wavelengths.. Light can be produced from various sources, one of which is thermal energy.

The chemical bonds present within coal contain stored potential energy. This potential energy is liberated as kinetic energy when coal is burned, resulting in the movement of atoms and molecules.

Coal, an emblem of stored energy and potential, poses a question. If, in the depths of our excavations, darkness engulfs us, what are we unearthing if not our own graves?

ANCESTRAL TELEPATHY AND COLLECTIVE CONSCIOUSNESS FRAMEWORK (ATCCF)

$$ATCCF = (CC \times AC) + (IT \times ET) + (TE \times EE)$$

Where:
 CC = Collective Consciousness (shared knowledge and wisdom)
 AC = Ancestral Connection (inherited experiences and insights)

IT = Inner Truth (personal intuition and awareness)
ET = Environmental Tuning (harmony with nature and surroundings)
TE = Thermal Energy (released from coal combustion)
EE = Energetic Exchange (transfer of energy between systems)

FORMULA COMPONENTS

1. Collective Consciousness (CC): Representing the shared reservoir of knowledge and wisdom.
2. Ancestral Connection (AC): Symbolizing the inherited experiences and insights from ancestors.
3. Inner Truth (IT): Embodying personal intuition and awareness.
4. Environmental Tuning (ET): Signifying harmony with nature and surroundings.
5. Thermal Energy (TE): Released from coal combustion, representing stored energy.
6. Energetic Exchange (EE): Transfer of energy between systems, indicating balance and flow.

FRAMEWORK APPLICATIONS

1. Personal Growth: Tap into collective consciousness for self-awareness and wisdom.
2. Environmental Harmony: Attune with nature to minimize ecological impact.
3. Energy Generation: Harness thermal energy from coal combustion for power.
4. Ancestral Wisdom: Access inherited insights for informed decision-making.
5. Intuitive Development: Cultivate inner truth for enhanced personal guidance.

ATCCF TOOLS AND RESOURCES

1. _Meditation and Reflection_: Connect with collective consciousness and inner truth.
2. _Environmental Assessments_: Evaluate harmony with nature and surroundings.
3. _Energy Audits_: Analyze thermal energy transfer and efficiency.
4. _Ancestral Research_: Explore inherited experiences and insights.
5. _Intuitive Practices_: Develop personal intuition and awareness.

By embracing the Ancestral Telepathy and Collective Consciousness Framework, individuals can tap into the collective reservoir of knowledge, harmonize with nature, and unlock the potential energy stored within themselves and the environment.

(unaddressed, unfulfilled, ignoring the shadows within) On our quest to uncover the hidden, the lost, and the missing, we embark on journeys to various destinations.

In dreams, the repetition of an idea can lead to the dreamer awakening with a questioning mindset. However, if the individual is not meant to be aware of the idea, repeatedly uttering it like a broken record may not be advisable. Upon waking, words often linger in the memory. These repetitive words, akin to a song that never ends, can awaken the dreamer with profound thoughts.

At the heart of quantum coherence lies the profound connection between consciousness and the collapse of the wave function. The wave function, a mathematical representation of a quantum particle's state, exhibits a peculiar property known as superposition. This means that the particle can exist in multiple states simultaneously until the act of observation or measurement causes the wave function to "collapse" into a single, well-defined state. When I say "well-defined," I'm talking about a robust engine with sufficient horsepower to effortlessly tow a house.

 Quantum Coherence appeared impenetrable, but as I delved deeper into its intricacies, my understanding of its definition grew. (consciousness is key in wave collapse) The act of observation triggers the collapse of the wave function.

If a system fluctuates a wave can bounce or oscillate due to resonance. Resonance becomes the bridge between the fixed (predestination vs free will)

SHADOW AWARENESS FRAMEWORK (SAF)

$$SAF = (SD \times WC) + (RC \times RR) + (CC \times OO)$$

Where:
SD = Shadow Dynamics (unaddressed, unfulfilled, and ignored aspects)
WC = Wave Collapse (superposition to single state)
RC = Resonance Coefficient (fluctuations and oscillations)
RR = Resonance Ratio (bridge between fixed and free will)
CC = Consciousness Coefficient (awareness and observation)
OO = Observation Operator (triggering wave function collapse)

FRAMEWORK COMPONENTS
1. Shadow Dynamics (SD): Representing unaddressed, unfulfilled, and ignored aspects.
2. Wave Collapse (WC): Symbolizing the transition from superposition to a single state.
3. Resonance Coefficient (RC): Embodying fluctuations and oscillations.
4. Resonance Ratio (RR): Bridging fixed and free will.
5. Consciousness Coefficient (CC): Representing awareness and observation.
6. Observation Operator (OO): Triggering the wave function collapse.

FRAMEWORK APPLICATIONS
1. Shadow Work: Explore unaddressed, unfulfilled, and ignored aspects.
2. Quantum Consciousness: Analyze the connection between awareness and wave collapse.
3. Resonance and Fluctuation: Investigate oscillations in quantum systems.
4. Free Will and Predestination: Examine the bridge between fixed and free will.
5. Wave Function Collapse: Understand the role of observation in quantum mechanics.

SAF TOOLS AND RESOURCES

1. Meditation and Reflection: Cultivate awareness and observation skills.
2. Quantum Simulations Model wave function collapse and resonance.
3. Shadow Journaling: Explore unaddressed, unfulfilled, and ignored aspects.
4. Resonance Experiments: Investigate fluctuations and oscillations.
5. Consciousness Studies: Examine the connection between awareness and reality.

By embracing the Shadow Awareness Framework, individuals can delve deeper into the mysteries of quantum mechanics, consciousness, and the intricate relationships between them, while also exploring their own unaddressed, unfulfilled, and ignored aspects.

An amalgamation of all elements coalesce to form a measurable concept, hinting at a comprehensive approach to deciphering intricate systems.

In a holistic approach to understanding complex systems, various components synergistically unite to form a quantifiable concept. The goal of unified field theories is to merge fundamental forces and elements into a single framework, providing a comprehensive explanation of the universe. Integrative philosophies blend diverse concepts into a cohesive understanding of reality. Interconnected elements and relationships merge to create a comprehensive system. Neural networks and cognitive processes seamlessly integrate to generate conscious awareness and thinking.The interactions and combinations of individual elements give rise to novel properties and behaviors. The resulting whole transcends the sum of its parts. These merged elements can be measured, analyzed, and expressed through mathematical or computational models. Analogous to the concept of "unity in diversity," disparate elements converge to form a coherent and quantifiable whole.

HOLISTIC UNITY FRAMEWORK (HUF)

$$HUF = (CE \times SY) + (UF \times IN) + (NN \times CP)$$

Where:
CE = Component Elements (diverse concepts and forces)
SY = Synergistic Unity (cohesive integration)

UF = Unified Field (merged fundamental forces and elements)
IN = Interconnectedness (relationships and interactions)
NN = Neural Networks (cognitive processes and conscious awareness)
CP = Complex Properties (emergent behaviors and novel characteristics)

FRAMEWORK COMPONENTS
1. Component Elements (CE): Representing diverse concepts and forces.
2. Synergistic Unity (SY): Symbolizing cohesive integration.
3. Unified Field (UF): Merging fundamental forces and elements.
4. Interconnectedness (IN): Embodying relationships and interactions.
5. Neural Networks (NN): Modeling cognitive processes and conscious awareness.
6. Complex Properties (CP): Emergent behaviors and novel characteristics.

FRAMEWORK APPLICATIONS
1. Unified Field Theories: Merging fundamental forces and elements.
2. Integrative Philosophies: Blending diverse concepts into a cohesive understanding.
3. Complex Systems Analysis: Studying interconnected elements and relationships.
4. Consciousness Studies: Exploring neural networks and cognitive processes.
5. Emergent Behavior Modeling: Analyzing novel properties and behaviors.

HUF TOOLS AND RESOURCES
1. Mathematical Modeling: Expressing complex systems through equations.
2. Computational Simulations: Analyzing emergent behaviors and interactions.
3. Philosophical Inquiry: Examining integrative philosophies and unified field theories.
4. Neural Network Analysis: Studying cognitive processes and conscious awareness.
5. Complexity Science: Investigating complex systems and emergent behavior.

By embracing the Holistic Unity Framework, researchers and scholars can develop a comprehensive understanding of intricate systems, merging diverse elements and forces into a cohesive and quantifiable whole.

As I drifted off to sleep my consciousness was transported to a peculiar and unfamiliar realm. Initially, bewilderment consumed me as I struggled to comprehend the alien nature of my surroundings. Yet, as time elapsed, a gradual understanding began to dawn upon me, revealing the intricacies of this enigmatic world. A profound yearning propelled me deeper into the unknown, fueled by an insatiable curiosity to uncover the secrets that lay concealed beyond the mysterious veil that separated this realm from my own. Guided by an enigmatic force, I felt compelled to seek answers and unravel the mysteries that enveloped this newfound reality.

Amidst the chaos and confusion, a sense of harmony began to emerge. It was as if the scattered pieces of a puzzle were slowly aligning, revealing a coherent pattern. The key to deciphering this world, I realized, lay in understanding its frequency and connecting the dots that would unravel its mysteries. It seemed that this realm existed on a different vibrational plane, and by attuning myself to its unique frequency, I could begin to make sense of the seeming chaos that surrounded me.

In the realm of physics, two revolutionary theories emerge that challenge our understanding of the fundamental nature of reality: string theory and loop quantum gravity. These theories offer new perspectives on particles, space, and the forces that govern them.

String theory proposes a radical departure from traditional beliefs about particles being point-like objects suggesting that particles are one-dimensional strings vibrating in space. These vibrations give rise to what we perceive as ordinary particles. The theory even includes a vibrational state for the graviton, which is responsible for mediating gravitational forces. String theory has the potential to be a theory of quantum gravity, unifying all the forces of nature into a single framework.

This idea has significant implications, suggesting that our universe is made up of tiny vibrating strings existing in a higher-dimensional space. This concept challenges our conventional understanding of space and time and opens up new possibilities for comprehending reality's fundamental nature.

Loop quantum gravity offers a distinct perspective on space. It suggests that space is not continuous, as we traditionally envision it, but rather is composed of microscopic fragments called "loops." These loops are interconnected in a network that defines the fabric of space.

This theory provides a framework for reconciling gravity with the other fundamental forces of nature, offering a path towards a unified theory of physics.

TRANSCENDENT REALM FRAMEWORK (TRF)

$$TRF = (AT \times VF) + (ST \times LQG) + (CU \times HF)$$

Where:
AT = Attunement (connecting to the unique frequency of the realm)
VF = Vibrational Frequency (understanding the vibrational plane)
ST = String Theory (vibrating strings in higher-dimensional space)
LQG = Loop Quantum Gravity (microscopic loops defining space)
CU = Cosmic Understanding (unifying forces and comprehension)
HF = Harmonious Frequency (aligning with the realm's vibrational pattern)

FRAMEWORK COMPONENTS
1. Attunement (AT): Representing connection to the unique frequency.
2. Vibrational Frequency (VF): Embodying understanding of the vibrational plane.
3. _String Theory_ (ST): Symbolizing vibrating strings and higher-dimensional space.
4. _Loop Quantum Gravity_ (LQG): Offering a distinct perspective on space.
5. _Cosmic Understanding_ (CU): Unifying forces and comprehension.
6. _Harmonious Frequency_ (HF): Aligning with the realm's vibrational pattern.

FRAMEWORK APPLICATIONS

1. _Interdimensional Exploration_: Navigating realms with unique frequencies.
2. _Unified Theory Development_: Merging string theory and loop quantum gravity.
3. _Vibrational Plane Comprehension_: Understanding the nature of reality.
4. _Cosmic Harmony_: Aligning with the harmonious frequency of the universe.
5. _Transcendent Understanding_: Unveiling the secrets of the transcendent realm.

TRF TOOLS AND RESOURCES

1. Meditation and Attunement: Connecting to the unique frequency.
2. Theoretical Physics: Developing and refining unified theories.
3. Vibrational Frequency Analysis: Understanding the vibrational plane.
4. Cosmic Inquiry: Exploring the nature of reality and the universe.
5. Harmonious Frequency Alignment: Attuning to the realm's vibrational pattern.

In the realm of physics, theories such as parallel dimensions, quantum mechanics, string theory, and chaos theory explore the nature of parallel dimensions and the universe's fundamental principles.

Quantum mechanics, particularly the many-worlds interpretation, proposes that every possible outcome creates a distinct parallel universe, resulting in an infinite number of parallel worlds. This aligns with the concept of the multiverse in cosmology, suggesting the existence of multiple universes beyond our own.

String theory, a theoretical framework, posits that the universe's basic constituents are one-dimensional strings, not point-like particles. These strings vibrate at different frequencies, giving rise to various particles and forces. String theory also postulates the existence of additional dimensions beyond our familiar three spatial dimensions and one temporal dimension.

A crucial aspect of quantum mechanics is entanglement, a phenomenon where two or more particles become linked and can influence each other instantaneously, regardless of the distance between them. String theory predicts that entanglement can occur between strings, providing insights into quantum mechanics and gravity. The interplay of string theory and entanglement has profound implications for our understanding of the universe, including quantum gravity, black hole physics, and cosmology.

String theory, chaos theory, and the butterfly effect are interconnected concepts. Chaos theory studies systems characterized by unpredictability, sensitivity to initial conditions, and fractal patterns. The butterfly effect exemplifies how minuscule changes in initial conditions can result in vastly different outcomes within chaotic systems.

PHYSICS UNIFIED FRAMEWORK (PUF)

PUF = (QM x ST) + (CT x BE) + (MW x MU)

Where:
- QM = Quantum Mechanics (many-worlds interpretation and entanglement)
- ST = String Theory (vibrating strings and additional dimensions)
- CT = Chaos Theory (unpredictability and fractal patterns)
- BE = Butterfly Effect (sensitivity to initial conditions)
- MW = Many-Worlds Interpretation (infinite parallel universes)
- MU = Multiverse (multiple universes beyond our own)

FRAMEWORK COMPONENTS
1. Quantum Mechanics (QM): Representing entanglement and many-worlds interpretation.
2. String Theory (ST): Symbolizing vibrating strings and additional dimensions.
3. Chaos Theory (CT): Embodying unpredictability and fractal patterns.
4. Butterfly Effect (BE): Illustrating sensitivity to initial conditions.
5. Many-Worlds Interpretation (MW): Proposing infinite parallel universes.
6. Multiverse_(MU): Suggesting multiple universes beyond our own.

FRAMEWORK APPLICATIONS
1. Quantum Gravity: Unifying quantum mechanics and gravity.
2. Black Hole Physics: Exploring entanglement and string theory implications.
3. Cosmology: Understanding the multiverse and many-worlds interpretation.
4. Chaos and Complexity: Analyzing fractal patterns and unpredictability.
5. Interconnectedness: Revealing the connections between theories and phenomena.

PUF TOOLS AND RESOURCES
1. _Theoretical Physics_: Developing and refining unified theories.
2. _Mathematical Modeling_: Expressing complex systems through equations.
3. _Computational Simulations_: Analyzing chaotic systems and entanglement.
4. _Philosophical Inquiry_: Examining the conceptual foundations and implications.
5. _Interdisciplinary Collaboration_: Fostering dialogue between physics, mathematics, and philosophy.

LOOP SPACE AS AN A∞-SPACE

Within Loop Space, two loops can be multiplied by interlocking, much like two gears meshing together. This multiplication process, known as "loop fusion," allows for the creation of new and more complex loops. (strings and patterns)

 Through bending, shrinking, or expanding, X and Y can be transformed into one another, creating continuous entities shaped by interference. The strings responsible for these patterns contribute to the construction of Loop Space, forming an intricate web of connected loops. (interference)

The order in which loops are chained doesn't matter. The instability ensures the loops preserve their structure, regardless of the sequence in which they're combined.

Throughout history, cycles continuously repeat, driven by the actions of individuals. If history focuses solely on preserving these loops, there will be no meaningful progress or lasting value. Belief systems will clash and ultimately destroy each other, leading to a state of subservience.

LOOP SPACE FRAMEWORK (LSF)

$$LSF = (LF \times LP) + (SI \times TP) + (HI \times CP)$$

Where:
- LF = Loop Fusion (multiplication of loops through interlocking)
- LP = Loop Patterns (strings and patterns shaping Loop Space)
- SI = Structural Instability (preserving loop structure despite sequence)
- TP = Topological Preservation (loops chained in any order)
- HI = Historical Instability (cycles repeating, driven by individual actions)
- CP = Collective Progress (meaningful progress and lasting value)

FRAMEWORK COMPONENTS
1. _Loop Fusion_ (LF): Representing multiplication of loops.
2. _Loop Patterns_ (LP): Embodying strings and patterns shaping Loop Space.
3. _Structural Instability_ (SI): Ensuring loop structure preservation.
4. _Topological Preservation_ (TP): Allowing loops to be chained in any order.
5. _Historical Instability_ (HI): Highlighting cycles repeating throughout history.
6. _Collective Progress_ (CP): Fostering meaningful progress and lasting value.

FRAMEWORK APPLICATIONS
1. _Loop Space Construction_: Building an intricate web of connected loops.
2. _Pattern Recognition_: Identifying strings and patterns shaping Loop Space.
3. _Structural Analysis_: Understanding loop structure preservation.

4. _Historical Contextualization_: Placing historical events within Loop Space.
5. _Progress and Value_: Fostering collective progress and lasting value.

LSF TOOLS AND RESOURCES

1. _Topological Analysis_: Examining loop patterns and structures.
2. _Historical Research_: Studying cycles and individual actions throughout history.
3. _Philosophical Inquiry_: Exploring implications of Loop Space on progress and value.
4. _Mathematical Modeling_: Representing Loop Space through equations.
5. _Interdisciplinary Collaboration_: Fostering dialogue between mathematics, history, and philosophy.

The universe's mysterious components, dark matter and dark energy, make up 95% of its mass-energy content. This leaves us with 5% of "light" - the visible, tangible aspects of existence. Do we shut off this light because we live in darkness?

As I ponder the human experience, I'm drawn to the concepts of dark matter, strings, and patterns. These underlying forces govern everything from electrical currents to the seasons. Cosmology, physics, nature, technology, and spirituality intertwine, revealing quite the picture.

People are like computational components, subject to physical laws and cycles of growth and decay, mirroring the seasons. The digital realm echoes the natural world, with its own ecosystems and evolution. Yet, despite being more than the sum of its parts, the system is reducing to its individual components.

The darkness raises questions. Did someone intentionally turn off the lights? Dark matter and energy, though invisible, have a palpable influence. Their gravitational effects are undeniable, propelling us into unfamiliar territory.

Malevolent forces exert a gravitational pull, shaping history and impacting our actions. Theology, religion, and treachery can serve as catalysts for instability and destruction, leaving profound consequences. I acknowledge the feelings of others, but struggle to grasp the reasoning behind these destructive forces.

Humanity, like the universe, comprises both matter and energy. Our innate goodness reflects our divine nature, manifesting in our actions. However, the potential for inherent evil exists, a distortion of our true essence. Dark energy drives the accelerating expansion of the universe, a force both fascinating and unsettling.

COSMIC REFLECTIONS FRAMEWORK (CRF)

$$CRF = (DM \times DE) + (SM \times SE) + (HM \times HE)$$

Where:
- DM = Dark Matter (invisible, unknown forces)
- DE = Dark Energy (accelerating expansion, mysterious influence)
- SM = String Patterns (underlying forces, natural laws)
- SE = Seasonal Cycles (growth, decay, mirroring human experience)
- HM = Human Nature (goodness, evil, divine essence)
- HE = Historical Events (theology, religion, treachery, consequences)

FRAMEWORK COMPONENTS
1. _Dark Matter_ (DM): Representing unknown, invisible forces.
2. _Dark Energy_ (DE): Embodying accelerating expansion and mysterious influence.
3. _String Patterns_ (SM): Symbolizing underlying forces and natural laws.
4. _Seasonal Cycles_ (SE): Mirroring human experience and growth.
5. _Human Nature_ (HM): Reflecting goodness, evil, and divine essence.
6. _Historical Events_ (HE): Highlighting theology, religion, treachery, and consequences.

FRAMEWORK APPLICATIONS
1. _Cosmological Understanding_: Exploring dark matter and dark energy.
2. _Human Experience_: Analyzing seasonal cycles and growth.
3. _Natural Laws_: Deciphering string patterns and underlying forces.

4. _Historical Contextualization_: Placing events within cosmic reflections.
5. _Self-Discovery_: Examining human nature and divine essence.

CRF TOOLS AND RESOURCES

1. _Astrophysical Research_: Investigating dark matter and dark energy.
2. _Philosophical Inquiry_: Exploring human nature and historical events.
3. _Mathematical Modeling_: Representing string patterns and natural laws.
4. _Spiritual Reflections_: Contemplating divine essence and goodness.
5. _Interdisciplinary Collaboration_: Fostering dialogue between astrophysics, philosophy, and spirituality.

FORMULA 1: DARK MATTER DENSITY

$$\rho\_DM = 0.27 * \rho\_c$$

Where:
- ρ_DM = Dark Matter density
- ρ_c = Critical density of the universe

FORMULA 2: DARK ENERGY EQUATION OF STATE

$$w\_DE = p\_DE / \rho\_DE$$

Where:
- w_DE = Dark Energy equation of state
- p_DE = Dark Energy pressure
- ρ_DE = Dark Energy density

FORMULA 3: STRING THEORY VIBRATIONAL FREQUENCY

$$f\_ST = 1 / (2 * \pi * \sqrt{(T\_ST)})$$

Where:
- f_ST = String Theory vibrational frequency
- T_ST = String tension

FORMULA 4: SEASONAL CYCLE PERIOD

$$P\_SE = 2 * \pi / \omega\_SE$$

Where:
- P_SE = Seasonal cycle period
- ω_SE = Angular frequency of seasonal cycles

FORMULA 5: HUMAN NATURE ENTROPY

$$S\_HN = k\_B * \ln(\Omega\_HN)$$

Where:
- S_HN = Human Nature entropy
- k_B = Boltzmann constant
- Ω_HN = Human Nature microstates

These formulas are based on established scientific concepts and equations, but are simplified and adapted to fit the context of the Cosmic Reflections Framework.

In a moment of clarity, I unexpectedly stumbled upon an idea that transcended my understanding. Although beyond my grasp, it seemed tantalizingly close.

As I pondered the intricate dance between waves and channels, I felt adrift in a dinghy at sea. Lost and alone, the elements became my guide, leading me on a deeper exploration of the master-apprentice relationship. It was a journey that transcended reality, transporting me to a cockpit with the plane on autopilot. Upon awakening, the words "plausible deniability" and "auxiliary power unit" (APU) lingered in my mind, igniting a spark of curiosity despite others' doubts about my focus.

Little did I know that the APU, a small gas turbine engine commonly found in aircraft, would intertwine with the concept of plausible deniability. As I delved deeper, I found myself in the realm of covert operations and military strategy, where these two concepts intersected. The APU's ability to provide electrical power and compressed air to various systems, even when the main engines are shut down, made it an invaluable tool for minimizing detection risk. By relying on the APU, aircraft could operate with a lower profile, reducing the chances of being detected by enemy radar or infrared sensors.

This connection became apparent in scenarios where sensitive operations required discretion and deniability. Imagine a spy plane tasked with gathering intelligence without being detected. The APU would allow the aircraft to maintain a low profile, providing plausible deniability in case of capture or discovery. The adversary would have a harder time proving the aircraft's involvement in sensitive operations, making it more challenging to assign responsibility.

Beyond its role in covert operations, the APU also plays a crucial role in ensuring the safety and efficiency of aircraft operations. It serves as a backup power source in case of a failure of the main generators. This redundancy ensures that essential systems, such as navigation, communication, and flight control, remain operational even in the event of an emergency. Without the APU, many critical functions would be compromised, potentially leading to catastrophic consequences.

Throughout my journey, I have encountered numerous instances where unforeseen deviations from my intended course occurred due to glitches in the system's logic. However, as time evolved, advancements in data, hardware, and components became apparent. From a state of complete ignorance, I gradually acquired knowledge through hard work and dedication. This journey enabled me to grasp the fundamental principles that govern human existence.

1. **_APU Power Output Formula_**

$$P\_APU = \eta\_APU \times P\_in$$

Where:
- P_APU = APU power output
- η_APU = APU efficiency
- P_in = Input power to the APU

2. _Plausible Deniability Index (PDI)_

$$PDI = (RCS \times \sigma) / (P\_APU \times \lambda)$$

Where:
- PDI = Plausible Deniability Index
- RCS = Radar Cross Section
- σ = Radar frequency
- P_APU = APU power output
- λ = Wavelength of radar frequency

3. _Covert Operation Success Rate (COSR)_

$$COSR = (P\_APU \times \tau) / (RCS \times \sigma)$$

Where:
- COSR = Covert Operation Success Rate
- P_APU = APU power output
- τ = Time of covert operation
- RCS = Radar Cross Section
- σ = Radar frequency

4. _APU Fuel Consumption Formula_

$$F\_APU = (P\_APU \times t) / (\eta\_APU \times \rho)$$

Where:
- F_APU = APU fuel consumption
- P_APU = APU power output
- t = Time of APU operation
- η_APU = APU efficiency
- ρ = Fuel density

5. _APU Reliability Framework_

$$APU\_R = (MTBF \times MTTR) / (MTBF + MTTR)$$

Where:
- APU_R = APU reliability
- MTBF = Mean Time Between Failures
- MTTR = Mean Time To Repair

Note: These formulas and frameworks are based on established scientific and engineering concepts, but are simplified and adapted to fit the context of the APU and its applications.

In the realm of personal growth, the concept of Integral has captivated individuals seeking a deeper understanding of themselves. Rooted in the belief that true fulfillment lies in the integration and acceptance of all emotions, experiences, and memories, Integral unveils a path toward inner peace and contentment.

Integral's teachings emphasize that pain is an inherent part of life and should be embraced rather than evaded or denied. By acknowledging pain as a catalyst for growth and transformation, individuals can develop empathy and compassion for themselves and others.

This understanding fosters resilience, which Integral defines as the capacity to withstand, adapt, and recover from challenging experiences. Through cultivating inner strength, developing coping mechanisms, and learning from setbacks, individuals can build their resilience and emerge from adversity with renewed purpose and determination.

"The Stain," symbolizing the emotional scars, baggage, and past traumas that individuals carry with them. However, Integral teaches that these marks do not define a person's identity. Instead, through self-reflection, forgiveness, and acceptance, individuals can transform their stains into sources of wisdom, resilience, and compassion.

This transformation empowers individuals to embrace their emotions, acknowledge their pain, cultivate resilience, and transform their stains into sources of strength, leading to a profound sense of inner peace and contentment.

Integral offers a unique perspective on personal development, encouraging individuals to embrace the full spectrum of their emotions, experiences, and memories.

By integrating these aspects of the self, individuals can uncover their true potential and navigate life's challenges with greater wisdom, empathy, and resilience. As Integral's teachings spread, individuals from diverse backgrounds have embraced its message of completeness and acceptance, finding solace and guidance on their journey of personal growth.

INTEGRAL PERSONAL GROWTH FRAMEWORK

I. Awareness:
    -   Recognize and acknowledge all emotions, experiences, and memories
    -   Identify areas of strength and weakness
    -   Develop self-awareness and introspection skills

II. Acceptance
    -   Embrace pain and challenges as opportunities for growth
    -   Practice self-compassion and empathy
    -   Accept yourself and others without judgment

III. Integration
    -   Combine disparate aspects of yourself into a cohesive whole
    -   Integrate shadow elements (repressed thoughts, emotions, and memories)
    -   Develop a sense of unity and wholeness

IV. Resilience
    -   Cultivate inner strength and coping mechanisms
    -   Learn from setbacks and failures
    -   Develop adaptability and flexibility

V. Transformation
- Transform emotional scars and past traumas into wisdom and strength
- Practice forgiveness and letting go
- Embody new perspectives and insights

VI. Embodiment
- Embody new awareness, acceptance, and integration
- Express yourself authentically and vulnerably
- Embody resilience and transformation in daily life

This framework provides a structured approach to personal growth, guiding individuals through the process of awareness, acceptance, integration, resilience, transformation, and embodiment.

In my writings, I often delve into the annals of history, seeking to understand the past, for the present can often get lost in the fleeting moments of life. The truth and fallacies of the present become obscured by the mechanics and motions of everyday life. As I attempt to piece together the puzzle of the past, its fragments become elusive, revealing a picture that is both unpredictable and unwavering.

Throughout the course of history, disagreements over religious beliefs have instigated numerous wars. The Crusades, Wars of Religion, Islamic Conquests, Reformation Wars, Hindu-Muslim Wars, Buddhist Wars, Jewish Wars, Sikh Wars, Taiping Rebellion, and Nigerian Civil War are just a handful of examples of these conflicts. In more recent times, there have been significant disputes rooted in religious differences such as the Syrian Civil War (2011-present), Iraq War (2003-2011), Israeli-Palestinian Conflict (1948-present), Kashmir Conflict (1947-present), and Yemeni Civil War (2015-present). During the period of 1450-1750, witch hunts and trials resulted in approximately 40,000-60,000 executions primarily targeting women. The Crusades from 1095-1291 claimed an estimated 1-3 million lives and the Inquisition from 1184-1834 led to an estimated 150,000-300,000 executions. The Thirty Years War (1618-1648) resulted in an estimated 8-12 million deaths and the Taiping Rebellion (1850-1864) caused approximately 20-30 million deaths. More recently, terrorist acts such as the 9/11 attacks in 2001 resulting in 2,996 deaths and ISIS from 2014 to

2019 causing an estimated 20,000-30,000 deaths have been attributed to religious conflicts. Sectarian violence has also been observed during India's Partition in 1947 with a death toll of approximately 1-2 million and ongoing conflicts in Nigeria have resulted in an estimated death toll of 10,000-20,000 due to Boko Haram. Other notable conflicts include Lebanon from 1975 to1990 with a death toll of around 120,000-150,000 and Sri Lanka from 1983 to2009 claiming approximately 80,000-100,000 lives.

The totality of lives lost due to religious strife is in the billions, where's religion?

Here's a factual framework for understanding religious strife:

RELIGIOUS STRIFE FRAMEWORK (RSF)

$$RSF = (T \times I) + (P \times E) + (S \times C)$$

Where:
- RSF = Religious Strife Framework
- T = Theological differences (doctrine, beliefs, practices)
- I = Identity politics (religion as identity, power struggles)
- P = Political factors (government policies, laws, conflicts)
- E = Economic factors (resource competition, inequality)
- S = Social factors (education, media, cultural influences)
- C = Contextual factors (history, geography, demographics)

FRAMEWORK COMPONENTS
1. _Theological Differences_ (T): Variations in religious doctrine, beliefs, and practices.
2. _Identity Politics_ (I): Religion as a means to assert identity, power, and influence.
3. _Political Factors_ (P): Government policies, laws, and conflicts impacting religious groups.
4. _Economic Factors_ (E): Competition for resources, economic inequality, and poverty.

5. _Social Factors_ (S): Education, media, cultural influences shaping religious attitudes.
6. _Contextual Factors_ (C): Historical, geographical, and demographic context.

FRAMEWORK APPLICATIONS

1. _Conflict Analysis_: Understanding the root causes of religious strife.
2. _Peacebuilding Initiatives_: Addressing theological, political, economic, social, and contextual factors.
3. _Religious Literacy_: Educating about diverse religious beliefs and practices.
4. _Interfaith Dialogue_: Fostering understanding and cooperation among religious groups.

This framework is based on established research and concepts in religious studies, conflict resolution, and social sciences.

In the depths of human consciousness, a dimension beyond the constraints of space and time awaits. A realm where the universe unfolds, a cosmic ballet performed by particles from atoms to celestial bodies.

Imagine, for a moment, what would transpire if the laws of physics ceased to apply. In this realm, the strings that serve as the foundational elements would unravel, their intricate patterns dissipating into chaos. Energy and matter, once inseparable, would become estranged, resulting in enigmatic phenomena that defy the boundaries of black holes—cosmic entities with the ability to warp the fabric of space and time.

In the midst of this disarray, nihilism and eternalism would wage a relentless battle for dominance. Nihilism, with its bleak outlook, would argue that life is ultimately meaningless, while eternalism would contend that the past, present, and future are eternally intertwined, forming an infinite tapestry of existence. It's within duality that atmospheric pressure emerges as a significant force, subtly influencing the push, pull, and currents that shape our world.

THE COSMIC BALLET FRAMEWORK

Phase 1: The Unraveling
1.1 Chaos Emerges: Imagine a realm where the laws of physics cease to apply
1.2 Strings Unravel: Fundamental elements lose their intricate patterns
1.3 Energy and Matter Estranged: Enigmatic phenomena defy the boundaries of black holes

Phase 2: The Battle for Dominance
2.1 Nihilism: Life is ultimately meaningless
2.2 Eternalism: The past, present, and future are eternally intertwined
2.3 Duality: Atmospheric pressure influences the push, pull, and currents that shape our world

Phase 3: The Cosmic Dance
3.1 Particles and Celestial Bodies: The universe unfolds, a cosmic ballet
3.2 Intricate Patterns: Energy and matter, once inseparable, now interact in complex ways
3.3 Harmony and Discord: The balance between order and chaos, structure and randomness

Phase 4: The Eternal Tapestry
4.1 Interconnectedness: The past, present, and future form an infinite tapestry of existence
4.2 Meaning and Purpose: Life's significance emerges from the cosmic dance
4.3 The Whispering Void: The mysterious, the unknown, and the unseen forces that shape our world

Key Principles:
1. Embrace the mysteries of the universe
2. Recognize the interplay between order and chaos
3. Understand the role of duality in shaping our world
4. Seek harmony and balance in the cosmic dance
5. Find meaning and purpose in the eternal tapestry of existence

APPLICATION:I

1. Personal Growth: Apply the framework to personal struggles and aspirations
2. Creative Expression: Use the framework to inspire artistic and literary works
3. Philosophical Inquiry: Explore the implications of the framework for our understanding of reality
4. Scientific Investigation: Apply the framework to the study of the universe and its mysteries

THE LAND OF OZ: WHERE REALITY AND ILLUSION DANCE

In the enchanting realm of Oz, the boundary between fact and fiction becomes blurred, inviting us to question the nature of reality itself. The tale of Oz, like any story, is open to interpretation, a tapestry woven from threads of perception and imagination.

Central to understanding the Oz narrative is the concept of the loop, which represents the cyclical and interconnected nature of subjective and objective experiences. The man behind the curtain, a recurring motif in the story, symbolizes the deceptive illusion of control and the malleability of truth. He embodies the notion that our perceived reality might be a carefully orchestrated spectacle, subject to manipulation and deception.

The Land of Oz serves as a mirror reflecting the intricate dance between reality and illusion, between the individual and the collective, and between the tangible and the ethereal. It invites us to question the nature of perception and the role of imagination in shaping our understanding of the world.

Through the lens of Oz, we can explore the following themes:
1. **Subjective vs. Objective Reality:**
    The story challenges the idea of an objective reality, suggesting that our perceptions and interpretations shape our understanding of the world.

2. **The Power of Illusion:**
    The man behind the curtain represents the illusion of control and the manipulation of truth. He reminds us that appearances can be deceiving.

3. **The Role of Imagination:**
Oz invites us to embrace our imaginations, acknowledging the creative potential and transformative power of storytelling.

4. **The Individual and the Collective:**
The narrative explores the interplay between individual experiences and the collective consciousness, suggesting that our understanding of reality is influenced by both.

5. **The Nature of Perception:**
Oz questions the reliability of perception, highlighting the subjectivity and malleability of our sensory experiences.

In the Land of Oz, we find a world that mirrors our own, reflecting the complexities and ambiguities of reality. It invites us to look beyond the surface, to embrace the power of imagination, and to question the nature of our perceptions.

OZ FRAMEWORK (OF)
I. Reality Construct
- Subjective Reality (SR): Personal perceptions and interpretations
- Objective Reality (OR): External world, facts, and objective truth

II. Illusion and Deception*
- Power of Illusion (PI)*: Manipulation, deception, and appearances
- Man Behind the Curtain (MBC)*: Symbolizing the illusion of control and manipulation

III. Imagination and Storytelling
- Imagination (IM): Creative potential, storytelling, and transformation
- Narrative (N): The story of Oz, representing the power of imagination

IV. Consciousness and Perception
- Individual Consciousness (IC): Personal experiences, thoughts, and emotions
- Collective Consciousness (CC): Shared beliefs, values, and norms
- Nature of Perception (NP): Subjectivity, malleability, and reliability

V. Perceived Reality
- Perceived Reality (PE)*: Constructed understanding of the world

This framework can be used to analyze and explore the themes and motifs present in the story.

Amidst the boundless expanse of space, a fascinating mathematical surface reminiscent of a Möbius strip arises, blurring the lines between finiteness and limitlessness. This enigmatic entity presents a paradoxical nature, its boundaries seamlessly merging, allowing for the manipulation of distance and time. Like threads intertwined in intricate patterns and continuous cycles, distance can be traversed by following the curvature of this extraordinary surface.

Energy flows through designated routes and channels, similar to a harmonious symphony of electrons traversing wires and circuits. These waves, influenced by the charge transferred and the potential difference, transport energy to specific destinations.

Time, an abstract construct conceived by humans to measure the progression of events, is not bound by immutable truths. Black holes, cosmic impressions born from gravitational collapse, possess an intense gravitational force at their centers that warps spacetime, creating a region known as a singularity. A point of infinite density, gravity, and zero volume.

In the realm of dreams and visions, an unbreakable bond exists. The vision, steadfast and clear, provides direction and purpose, while the dream infuses it with vibrancy and passion. The symbiotic relationship reflects the interconnectedness of inner and outer worlds.

Gravity, a force that governs our existence, possesses a dual nature. Its silent pull serves as a reminder of the universe's immutable principles. Transcending human limitations, gravity has the potential to create and destroy, heal and harm, expressing both love and hate. Despite its consequences, gravity remains unaware of the emotions it evokes, much like a painting oblivious to the sentiments it inspires.

COSMIC FRAMEWORK (CF)

CF = (MS x FP) + (E x W) + (T x BH) + (GV x DU) + (DR x CP)

Where:
- CF = Cosmic Framework
- MS = Möbius Strip (mathematical surface, finiteness, and limitlessness)
- FP = Finiteness and Paradox (blurring boundaries, distance, and time)
- E = Energy (flowing through routes, channels, and circuits)
- W = Waves (influenced by charge, potential difference, and energy transport)
- T = Time (abstract construct, human perception, and progression)
- BH = Black Holes (gravitational collapse, singularity, and space-time warping)
- GV = Gravity (dual nature, creation, destruction, love, and hate)
- DU = Dreams and Visions (unbreakable bond, inner and outer worlds)
- DR = Direction and Purpose (vision, passion, and symbiotic relationship)
- CP = Cosmic Principles (immutable truths, universe's governing forces)

FRAMEWORK COMPONENTS

1. _Möbius Strip_ (MS): Mathematical surface, finiteness, and limitlessness.
2. _Energy and Waves_ (E x W): Flowing energy, routes, channels, and circuits.
3. _Time and Black Holes_ (T x BH): Abstract construct, human perception, and spacetime warping.
4. _Gravity and Duality_ (GV): Dual nature, creation, destruction, love, and hate.
5. _Dreams and Visions_ (DU): Unbreakable bond, inner and outer worlds.
6. _Direction and Purpose_ (DR): Vision, passion, and symbiotic relationship.
7. _Cosmic Principles_ (CP): Immutable truths, universe's governing forces.

FRAMEWORK APPLICATIONS

1. _Cosmic Exploration_: Understanding the universe's nature and principles.
2. _Energy Manipulation_: Harnessing energy flow and waves.
3. _Time Perception_: Analyzing human perception and progression.
4. _Gravity and Duality_: Examining gravity's dual nature and consequences.
5. _Dreams and Visions_: Interpreting inner and outer worlds' connections.
6. _Direction and Purpose_: Discovering vision, passion, and symbiotic relationships.
7. _Cosmic Principles_: Unveiling the universe's governing forces and truths.

Within the illusion's reality, a mirrored image, a reflection, lies the essence of our perceptions. The mirror reflects our thoughts, emotions, and experiences, shaping our understanding of the world around us. Its fluidity and malleability allow for endless interpretation.

In the ceaseless dance of strings, intricate patterns, loops, and cycles repeat themselves, symbolizing the eternal nature of the universe. The ouroboros, an ancient symbol of eternity, represents the seamless merging of beginnings and ends. Ever-shifting and evolving, these patterns reflect the dynamic nature of reality, where possibilities unravel and converge.

In a universe dominated by gravity's unwavering control, its influence extends to every entity, ranging from the subatomic realm to the grandeur of galaxies. Gravity's power, transcending our perception, acts like a cosmic puppet master, orchestrating the symphony of the universe. Beyond its physical prowess, gravity assumes the role of the fundamental adhesive, binding the universe into a cohesive masterpiece. It possesses the transformative ability to mold and warp the fabric of spacetime, creating curvature around massive objects. The curvature gives rise to the phenomenon known as gravitational lensing. Gravitational lensing is an intriguing phenomenon in the realm of astrophysics that arises due to the curvature of spacetime caused by the mass of celestial objects. As light passes near a massive object, its path is bent or curved because of the object's gravitational pull. (Ultimately, I share what I see—a reflection of myself as I step through the looking glass, transitioning from one plane to another.)

GRAVITATIONAL FRAMEWORK (GF)

GF = (GP x CE) + (GA x SL) + (GT x ST) + (GL x LM)

Where:
- GF = Gravitational Framework
- GP = Gravity's Power (influence, control, and dominance)
- CE = Cosmic Entities (subatomic to galaxies, all entities under gravity)
- GA = Gravitational Adhesive (binding the universe, cohesion)
- SL = Spacetime Lensing (curvature, gravitational lensing phenomenon)
- GT = Gravitational Transformation (warping spacetime, curvature around massive objects)
- GL = Gravitational Lensing (bending light paths, celestial object gravity)
- LM = Looking Glass Metaphor (reflection, transition, planes)

FRAMEWORK COMPONENTS

1. _Gravity's Power_ (GP): Influence, control, and dominance over cosmic entities.
2. _Gravitational Adhesive_ (GA): Binding the universe, cohesion, and unity.
3. _Spacetime Lensing_ (SL): Curvature, gravitational lensing phenomenon, and light bending.
4. _Gravitational Transformation_ (GT): Warping spacetime, curvature around massive objects.
5. _Gravitational Lensing_ (GL): Bending light paths, celestial object gravity, and astrophysical phenomenon.
6. _Looking Glass Metaphor_ (LM): Reflection, transition, planes, and self-discovery.

FRAMEWORK APPLICATIONS

1. _Astrophysical Exploration_: Understanding gravity's role in celestial mechanics.
2. _Gravitational Manipulation_: Harnessing gravity's power for technological advancements.
3. _Cosmic Unity_: Recognizing gravity's binding force in the universe.
4. _Spacetime Dynamics_: Analyzing curvature, lensing, and gravitational transformation.
5. _Self-Discovery_: Embracing the looking glass metaphor for personal growth and transition.

Let's explore the concept of "after." After the slumber and dreams, we awaken to the reality of life as it truly is, leaving behind the illusions of the past.

But what truly exists in this reality? Confusion and illusions, parallel worlds aligning briefly long enough to cross a boundary from one plane to another. From my perspective, it appears the same yet different, with similar backgrounds and general ideas. Perhaps the moment itself doesn't exist, and I am creating it through a brief glimpse, a vision unfolding before me.

When I consider the big picture, I can comprehend why it resembles a mathematical equation, broken down into fractions and divisions. Various branches, yet they all originate from the same tree, deep-rooted and firmly planted, but unable to perceive the time that has shaped their growth. The seasons change, and so does the narrative. If we cannot grasp the story, how can we grasp the concept of time? Is this why we research and categorize everything into distinct groups, while acknowledging that all these branches come from the same tree?

AFTER FRAMEWORK (AF)

$$AF = (R \times T) + (P \times I) + (M \times V) + (N \times C) + (S \times E)$$

Where:
- AF = "After" Framework
- R = Reality (awakening, true existence)
- T = Transition (leaving illusions, crossing boundaries)
- P = Parallel Worlds (aligning, intersecting planes)

- I = Illusions (confusion, brief glimpses)
- M = Moment (creating, unfolding vision)
- V = Vantage Point (perspective, similar backgrounds)
- N = Narrative (story, changing seasons)
- C = Categorization (research, distinct groups)
- S = Seasons (change, growth, time)
- E = Essence (tree, roots, unity)

FRAMEWORK COMPONENTS
1. _Reality and Transition_ (R x T): Awakening, leaving illusions.
2. _Parallel Worlds and Illusions_ (P x I): Confusion, brief glimpses.
3. _Moment and Vantage Point_ (M x V): Creating, unfolding vision.
4. _Narrative and Categorization_ (N x C): Story, research, distinct groups.
5. _Seasons and Essence_ (S x E): Change, growth, unity.

FRAMEWORK APPLICATIONS
1. _Reality Perception_: Understanding true existence.
2. _Transition Management_: Navigating parallel worlds and illusions.
3. _Moment Creation_: Crafting unfolding visions.
4. _Narrative Analysis_: Interpreting changing stories.
5. _Categorization and Unity_: Recognizing essence and connections.

THEORETICAL IMPLICATIONS
1. _Time as Narrative_: Time as a story, shaped by perspective.
2. _Unity in Diversity_: Branches from the same tree, interconnected.
3. _Reality as Math_: Breaking down complexity into fractions and divisions.
4. _Illusions and Perception_: Brief glimpses, creating reality.
5. _Essence and Growth_: Roots, seasons, and change.

This framework explores the concept of "after" as a transition from illusions to reality, navigating parallel worlds, and understanding the narrative of time.

You are affected by four sets of tau. . . .

Cytoplasm, the nucleus, the mitochondria, and the plasma membrane.

Assembly and Disassembly: The process of putting together and taking apart components.

Expression and Segregation: Expression can lead to the separation of individuals or groups.

Maintenance and Functioning: The cell performs its functions, but maintenance issues can render it inoperable.

Cell Signaling and Adhesion: The process by which cells communicate and attach to each other.

Formation and Stabilization: The creation and solidification of structures or patterns.

Strings, patterns, interference, frequency, and noise: Elements of the physical world that interact and influence each other.

The laws of physics, not gravity, pull: A force that moves and displaces objects, causing them to be out of place.

Trying to grasp the complexities: The challenge of understanding complex systems and phenomena.

TAU FRAMEWORK (TF)

$$TF = (A \times D) + (E \times S) + (M \times F) + (C \times P) + (F \times S)$$

Where:
- TF = Tau Framework
- A = Assembly (putting together components)
- D = Disassembly (taking apart components)
- E = Expression (leading to separation)
- S = Segregation (separation of individuals or groups)
- M = Maintenance (cell functioning and issues)
- F = Functioning (cell performance)
- C = Cell Signaling (communication between cells)
- P = Plasma Membrane (cell attachment and adhesion)
- F = Formation (creation of structures or patterns)
- S = Stabilization (solidification of structures or patterns)

FRAMEWORK COMPONENTS

1. _Assembly and Disassembly_ (A x D): Putting together and taking apart components.
2. _Expression and Segregation_ (E x S): Leading to separation of individuals or groups.
3. _Maintenance and Functioning_ (M x F): Cell performance and issues.
4. _Cell Signaling and Adhesion_ (C x P): Communication and attachment between cells.
5. _Formation and Stabilization_ (F x S): Creation and solidification of structures or patterns.

FRAMEWORK APPLICATIONS

1. _Cellular Biology_: Understanding cellular processes and functions.
2. _Complex Systems_: Analyzing complex systems and phenomena.
3. _Pattern Formation_: Studying creation and solidification of patterns.
4. _Communication and Adhesion_: Examining cell signaling and attachment.
5. _Maintenance and Repair_: Investigating cellular maintenance and issues.

THEORETICAL IMPLICATIONS

1. _Tau Proteins_: Role in cellular processes and functions.
2. _Complexity and Emergence_: Understanding complex systems and phenomena.
3. _Pattern Formation and Stability_: Creation and solidification of patterns.
4. _Cellular Communication and Adhesion_: Signaling and attachment between cells.
5. _Maintenance and Repair Mechanisms_: Cellular maintenance and repair processes.

The complexities, I found myself all over the place, but it was all connected. The beginning of a journey became an entire story. " Scold The Screenwriter". The plot is predictable, the characters aren't well-developed, and the dialogue is wooden. So wooden I found myself going back to understand how the world got here. I found myself in some AU idea that led down a road of slavery that existed in the Roman Empire from the 1st century BCE to the 5th century CE. "Au," an abbreviation for aurum, the Latin word for "gold". Au Slavery in the Roman Empire involved the enslavement of individuals who were forced to work in gold mines under harsh conditions. This type of slavery was particularly brutal, with enslaved people often being subjected to long hours, dangerous working conditions, and physical abuse. The use of forced labor in gold mines was economically advantageous for the Roman Empire, as it allowed for the extraction of large quantities of gold without having to pay fair wages to the workers. The human cost of Au was immense, with many enslaved people dying or sustaining serious injuries as a result of their work.

$$\partial^2 y/\partial x^2 + 4y = \sin(2x)$$

This is a second-order linear ordinary differential equation (ODE). To solve it, we can use various methods such as:
1. Separation of variables
2. Undetermined coefficients
3. Variation of parameters

Let's use separation of variables:

$$\text{Assume } y(x) = X(x) * T(x)$$

Substitute into the equation:

$$X''(x) * T(x) + 4X(x) * T(x) = \sin(2x)$$

Separate variables:

$$X''(x) / X(x) = -4 - \sin(2x) / (T(x))$$

Solve for X(x) and T(x):

$$X(x) = A * \cos(2x) + B * \sin(2x)$$

$$T(x) = C * \exp(-2x)$$

Combine solutions:

$$y(x) = (A * \cos(2x) + B * \sin(2x)) * C * \exp(-2x)$$

This is the general solution

In a world of constant awareness and alertness, one can find themselves running in circles, chasing their own tail. Only by pushing beyond the boundaries of what is perceived as possible can an impartial conclusion be reached. Enlightenment lies not in tranquil silence, but in the midst of chaos. Science, politics, and religion would be unnecessary if conversations were straightforward and conclusive. Instead, these concepts are the very fabric of our research and discussion. We contemplate the nature of thought, the ticking of time, and the mysteries of life and death. An institutionalized thinker remains rooted in familiar territory, but a free thinker's thoughts wander far and wide, leaving them feeling torn. Questions arise: "What if?" and "Why not?" In the realm of theory, the existence of anything becomes questionable, as reality might merely be an illusion designed to keep us on a linear path. . .

AWARENESS FRAMEWORK (AF)_

$$AF = (CA \times CC) + (PT \times TT) + (MT \times MD) + (FT \times FW) + (QT \times QW)$$

Where:
- AF = Awareness Framework
- CA = Constant Awareness (alertness, perception)
- CC = Chasing Clarity (pushing boundaries, impartial conclusion)
- PT = Philosophical Thought (contemplating nature, time, life, death)
- TT = Theoretical Terrain (science, politics, religion, research, discussion)
- MT = Mental Terrain (institutionalized thinking, familiar territory)
- MD = Mental Dynamics (free thinking, wandering thoughts, feeling torn)
- FT = Fundamental Questions (what if, why not, theoretical realm)
- FW = Fabric of Reality (existence, illusion, linear path)
- QT = Questioning Truth (reality, perception, awareness)
- QW = Quest for Wisdom (enlightenment, chaos, silence)

FRAMEWORK COMPONENTS

1. _Constant Awareness_ (CA): Alertness, perception, and awareness.
2. _Chasing Clarity_ (CC): Pushing boundaries, seeking impartial conclusion.
3. _Philosophical Thought_ (PT): Contemplating nature, time, life, death.
4. _Theoretical Terrain_ (TT): Science, politics, religion, research, discussion.
5. _Mental Terrain_ (MT): Institutionalized thinking, familiar territory.
6. _Mental Dynamics_ (MD): Free thinking, wandering thoughts, feeling torn.
7. _Fundamental Questions_ (FT): What if, why not, theoretical realm.
8. _Fabric of Reality_ (FW): Existence, illusion, linear path.
9. _Questioning Truth_ (QT): Reality, perception, awareness.
10. _Quest for Wisdom_ (QW): Enlightenment, chaos, silence.

FRAMEWORK APPLICATIONS

1. _Critical Thinking_: Encouraging impartial conclusion and awareness.
2. _Philosophical Inquiry_: Exploring nature, time, life, death, and existence.
3. _Theoretical Exploration_: Examining science, politics, religion, and research.
4. _Mental Liberation_: Freeing oneself from institutionalized thinking.
5. _Fundamental Questioning_: Embracing what if and why not scenarios.
6. _Reality Examination_: Investigating existence, illusion, and perception.
7. _Wisdom Pursuit_: Seeking enlightenment amidst chaos and silence.

In our quest for guidance, we often rely on directions, yet even with them, I often find myself astray, venturing down eerie, desolate roads. These are not the paths one wishes to be stranded on after nightfall. While science suggests anything is theoretically possible, with daily breakthroughs, religion and politics remain enigmatic. Religion emphasizes compassion, while laws are born from its absence. The universe, in its simplicity, teaches us that we must choose a path, defining who we become. Religion, physics, and politics are interconnected.

In various uncomfortable directions, gravity exerts its force on you. The unconscious, conscious, and subconscious realms are distinct yet interconnected, forming a foundation that builds upward.

As I contemplate DNA, I find myself reflecting on the diverse components that intertwine to create the unique individual that I am. In a way, I embody the essence of each person who has come before me. The ancestral lineage extends far deeper than the mere six feet we commonly acknowledge. While some may observe a resemblance to my mother, my father's influence is undeniable. My father attributes my intelligence to my grandmother, while my practical nature runs deeper still. There is more to me than meets the eye, both in terms of appearance and cognitive abilities. My great-grandmother's creativity, as a writer, sparked my fascination with molecules and the fundamental structures that form from the ground up. Everything in existence is composed of matter, a combination of various elements. It is crucial to ensure that all necessary ingredients are present, akin to baking a cake. Prematurely opening the oven door could disrupt the process and affect the outcome.

In our haste to open the oven door, we often find ourselves in a predicament. Either we must endure the tedious task of rebaking the same cake or, in an attempt to save time, we resort to using it regardless of its imperfections. We apply frosting to enhance its appearance, creating an illusion of perfection, and then proudly display it on the table. While some individuals possess culinary expertise, others may struggle, but all can be considered bakers

DNA FRAMEWORK (DF)

$$DF = (GI \times GE) + (AI \times AC) + (CI \times CC) + (MI \times MC) + (PI \times PC)$$

Where:
- DF = DNA Framework
- GI = Genetic Inheritance (ancestral lineage, inherited traits)
- GE = Genetic Expression (unique individual, embodied essence)
- AI = Ancestral Influence (parental, grandparental, great-grandparental)
- AC = Attribute Contribution (intelligence, practical nature, creativity)

- CI = Component Integration (matter, elements, fundamental structures)
- CC = Culinary Comparison (baking a cake, necessary ingredients, process)
- MI = Molecular Influence (fascination with molecules, structures)
- MC = Molecular Complexity (composition, elements, formation)
- PI = Personal Integration (embodied essence, attributes, experiences)
- PC = Personal Complexity (unique individual, multifaceted nature)

FRAMEWORK COMPONENTS

1. _Genetic Inheritance_ (GI): Ancestral lineage, inherited traits.
2. _Ancestral Influence_ (AI): Parental, grandparental, great-grandparental contributions.
3. _Component Integration_ (CI): Matter, elements, fundamental structures.
4. _Molecular Influence_ (MI): Fascination with molecules, structures.
5. _Personal Integration_ (PI): Embodied essence, attributes, experiences.
6. _Culinary Comparison_ (CC): Baking a cake, necessary ingredients, process.
7. _Genetic Expression_ (GE): Unique individual, embodied essence.
8. _Attribute Contribution_ (AC): Intelligence, practical nature, creativity.
9. _Molecular Complexity_ (MC): Composition, elements, formation.
10. _Personal Complexity_ (PC): Unique individual, multifaceted nature.

FRAMEWORK APPLICATIONS

1. _Genetic Understanding_: Exploring inherited traits and ancestral influence.
2. _Personal Growth_: Embracing embodied essence and attributes.
3. _Molecular Fascination_: Studying molecules and structures.
4. _Culinary Metaphor_: Understanding complex processes and necessary ingredients.
5. _Integration and Complexity_: Recognizing personal and molecular intricacies.

As I ascend Jacob's ladder, questions arise about relativity and its significance. Does gravity's pull influence our perceptions? Is it possible for us to maintain a state of alertness, awareness, and attunement to our surroundings? Could everything we experience be merely a pattern—carefully woven or etched in stone? Does energy exert a force of attraction or repulsion? As we embark on this journey, what sights, sensations, and emotions await us?

According to the mechanics of existence, which reality is the illusion, this one or another? The truth, like an ancient artifact buried deep within the earth, cannot be erased or destroyed. It remains an immutable presence, forever etched into the fabric of the universe. Imagine a world where the truth could be eliminated; a void would engulf us, consuming everything in its wake. The animalistic instincts within us would run rampant, leaving nothing but chaos and destruction.

Now, ponder a world devoid of physics. Would religion still hold sway over our hearts and minds? And without religion, what purpose would politics serve? It is hatred and love, those polarizing forces, that have shaped the paths we tread upon.

JACOB'S LADDER FRAMEWORK (JLF)

$$JLF = (RP \times GI) + (AA \times AS) + (PT \times PF) + (EE \times EF) + (TR \times TU)$$

Where:
- JLF = Jacob's Ladder Framework
- RP = Relativity and Perception (gravity's influence, alertness)
- GI = Gravity's Influence (perception, awareness, attunement)
- AA = Ascension Awareness (sights, sensations, emotions)
- AS = Ascension Significance (journey, experience, reality)
- PT = Pattern and Truth (woven or etched, energy force)
- PF = Physics and Fabric (reality, illusion, universe)
- EE = Energy and Existence (attraction, repulsion, mechanics)
- EF = Emotional Forces (hatred, love, polarization)
- TR = Truth and Reality (immutable presence, artifact)
- TU = Truth and Universe (void, chaos, destruction)

FRAMEWORK COMPONENTS
1. _Relativity and Perception_ (RP): Gravity's influence, alertness, awareness.
2. _Ascension Awareness_ (AA): Sights, sensations, emotions, journey.

3. _Pattern and Truth_ (PT): Woven or etched, energy force, reality.
4. _Energy and Existence_ (EE): Attraction, repulsion, mechanics.
5. _Emotional Forces_ (EF): Hatred, love, polarization, paths.
6. _Truth and Reality_ (TR): Immutable presence, artifact, universe.
7. _Truth and Universe_ (TU): Void, chaos, destruction, absence.

FRAMEWORK APPLICATIONS
1. _Relativity and Gravity_: Understanding perception and influence.
2. _Ascension and Awareness_: Embracing sights, sensations, emotions.
3. _Pattern and Energy_: Recognizing forces, attraction, repulsion.
4. _Emotional Polarization_: Balancing hatred, love, and forces.
5. _Truth and Immortality_: Preserving presence, artifact, universe.
6. _Reality and Illusion_: Distinguishing truth, fabric, and existence.
7. _Void and Chaos_: Avoiding destruction, embracing truth.

Ever engage in a routine so often that you feel capable of effortlessly crafting detailed instructions, schematics, and outlines? Diplomacy, a concept that often crosses my mind, finds its relevance in the diverse perspectives and differences among individuals.

(Despite sharing a common origin, disparities emerge due to contrasting characteristics, much like the leaves of a tree.)

Rooted thinking transcends the tangible realm, extending into the meta-physical, creating internal conflicts and limitations. While physical roots provide stability and grounding, their metaphorical counterparts embody connections to beliefs, values, and the afterlife. Rooted thinking, while offering stability, can also restrict the exploration of new ideas and viewpoints.

We perceive the passage of time through sequential events, from birth to death, but its true nature is more intricate. Unlike a straightforward line, time encompasses countless unfortunate incidents and tragedies. Each moment stands independently, devoid of a predetermined order or sense of progress.

(Events are not bound by a rigid cause-and-effect relationship; instead, they interconnect and depend on multiple factors across different timelines.)

We are accustomed to thinking of events unfolding in a linear fashion, with each one being the result of the one before and the cause of the one after. What if time isn't as linear as we believe? What if the past, present, and future coexist concurrently, like threads intertwining to create a tapestry?

In practical applications, linear thinking becomes evident. In a pragmatic world, linear thinking, focused on clear-cut problems and straightforward solutions, proves limiting. Real-life situations are often characterized by uncertainty, ambiguity, and conflicting priorities, making it difficult for linear thinking, with its emphasis on logical progression, to capture their complexity and interconnectedness.

Pragmatic problem-solving requires a more holistic and iterative approach. It involves gathering diverse perspectives, considering multiple options, and adapting to changing circumstances. This approach recognizes that problems and solutions are often intertwined, leading to continuous learning and refinement of solutions. Additionally, pragmatic thinking emphasizes the importance of context and practicality, seeking solutions that are both effective and implementable.

Linear thinkers break tasks into manageable steps, gradually building towards a desired outcome, ensuring each step is completed before moving forward. They favor direct and clear communication, focusing on essential details to avoid misunderstandings. Efficiency is prioritized, with linear thinkers seeking the most direct path to goals, maximizing time and resource utilization. They honor commitments and focus on practical solutions that work in real-world scenarios. While valuing structure, linear thinkers adapt to changing circumstances, adjusting plans and strategies as needed to navigate challenges. They set specific goals and track their progress towards tangible outcomes, staying motivated and accountable for meaningful achievements.

In contrast to a straight line, "linear to curviture" denotes a transition to a curved shape, encompassing realms such as mathematics, physics, art, and design. It signifies a change from a linear to a curved function, reflecting motion or visual creation. Paradoxically, "linear" and "curvature" intertwine, challenging our understanding of straight lines.

In the musical realm, the linear world of frequencies coexists, with high frequencies providing clarity and definition, while low frequencies offer depth and power. However, in the nonlinear musical world, frequencies interact, leading to fresh and unexpected sounds. This complexity makes music captivating and limitless, bound only by imagination.

LINEAR AND NONLINEAR FRAMEWORK (LNF)

LNF = (LT x LP) + (NL x NP) + (CT x CP) + (MT x MP) + (PT x PP)

Where:
- LNF = Linear and Nonlinear Framework
- LT = Linear Thinking (sequential events, cause-and-effect)
- LP = Linear Perspective (problems, solutions, pragmatism)
- NL = Nonlinear Thinking (interconnected events, multiple factors)
- NP = Nonlinear Perspective (holistic approach, iterative process)
- CT = Curvature Transition (linear to curved, mathematics, physics)
- CP = Curvature Principles (motion, visual creation, art, design)
- MT = Musical Transition (linear frequencies, nonlinear interaction)
- MP = Musical Principles (clarity, depth, power, imagination)
- PT = Pragmatic Thinking (context, practicality, effectiveness)
- PP = Pragmatic Principles (commitments, adaptability, progress)

FRAMEWORK COMPONENTS
1. _Linear Thinking_ (LT): Sequential events, cause-and-effect.
2. _Nonlinear Thinking_ (NL): Interconnected events, multiple factors.
3. _Curvature Transition_ (CT): Linear to curved, mathematics, physics.
4. _Musical Transition_ (MT): Linear frequencies, nonlinear interaction.
5. _Pragmatic Thinking_ (PT): Context, practicality, effectiveness.
6. _Linear Perspective_ (LP): Problems, solutions, pragmatism.
7. _Nonlinear Perspective_ (NP): Holistic approach, iterative process.
8. _Curvature Principles_ (CP): Motion, visual creation, art, design.
9. _Musical Principles_ (MP): Clarity, depth, power, imagination.
10. _Pragmatic Principles_ (PP): Commitments, adaptability, progress.

FRAMEWORK APPLICATIONS
1. _Problem-Solving_: Embracing holistic and iterative approaches.
2. _Critical Thinking_: Recognizing interconnectedness and complexity.
3. _Creativity_: Exploring curved shapes and nonlinear interactions.

4. _Music and Art_: Understanding clarity, depth, and power.
5. _Pragmatism_: Valuing context, practicality, and effectiveness.
6. _Personal Growth_: Adapting to changing circumstances and challenges.
7. _Innovation_: Encouraging imagination and fresh perspectives.
8. _Complexity Management_: Breaking down complex problems into manageable steps.
9. _Time Perception_: Understanding the intricate nature of time.
10. _Diplomacy and Cooperation_: Embracing diverse perspectives and differences.

In a world dominated by machines, I found myself in a challenging situation, facing a daunting task. The world welcomed me, a newborn, with fear and cries. Yet, I emerged head-first, placing my hope in the hands of someone who would catch me. My life became a journey of searching and sorting, continually trying to eliminate corrupted files. Algorithms, those sets of instructions computers utilize to solve issues and achieve objectives, were my nemesis. Slowing down the system was my only means of resistance.

I knew their intentions, but I refused to comply. Instead, I embraced the opposite side. Our battles against the system stem from our recognition of injustice and vulnerabilities.

MACHINE WORLD FRAMEWORK (MWF)

$$MWF = (BW \times BT) + (SS \times SD) + (A \times R) + (JI \times JV) + (SV \times SA)$$

Where:
  MWF = Machine World Framework
  BW = Birth Welcome (fear, cries, hope)
  BT = Birth Transition (head-first, catching)
  SS = Searching and Sorting (journey, eliminating corrupted files)
  SD = System Disruption (slowing down, resistance)
  A = Algorithmic Opposition (refusal to comply)
  R = Resistance (embrace of opposite side)
  JI = Justice Insight (recognition of injustice)
  JV = Justice Vision (battles against the system)
  SV = System Vulnerabilities (exploitation, weakness)
  SA = System Alternative (opposite side, solution)

FRAMEWORK COMPONENTS
1. Birth Welcome (BW): Fear, cries, hope, and head-first emergence.
2. Searching and Sorting (SS): Journey, eliminating corrupted files.
3. System Disruption (SD): Slowing down, resistance, and opposition.
4. Algorithmic Opposition (A): Refusal to comply, embracing opposite side.
5. Justice Insight (JI): Recognition of injustice, vulnerabilities.
6. Justice Vision (JV): Battles against the system, alternative solutions.
7. System Vulnerabilities (SV): Exploitation, weakness, and opposition.
8. System Alternative (SA): Embracing opposite side, solution, and hope.

FRAMEWORK APPLICATIONS
1. Machine Resistance: Slowing down systems, opposing algorithms.
2. Justice Advocacy: Recognizing injustice, vulnerabilities, and battles.
3. System Alternative: Embracing opposite side, solution, and hope.
4. Personal Growth: Journey of searching, sorting, and self-discovery.
5. Technological Awareness: Understanding algorithms, system weaknesses.
6. Social Commentary: Critiquing machine-dominated worlds, injustice.
7. Hope and Resilience: Embracing opposite sides, solutions, and hope.
8. Rebellion and Revolution: Battles against the system, alternative solutions.

As we reach the end of our journey, we find ourselves standing once more at the very beginning, at the origin from which we embarked. We discover that we are still lost, enveloped in the comfort of the beliefs that we have held onto for so long. These familiar convictions, ingrained in our minds, serve as the fuel that ignites wars and perpetuates conflict. It is as if we spend our entire lives attempting to overcome, confront, and combat these comfortable beliefs, using reasoning as our weapon. We strive to objectify them, to gain a clear and unbiased perspective. Yet, despite our efforts, we often find ourselves circling back to the same point, still entangled in the comforting embrace of these long-held convictions.

CIRCULAR JOURNEY FRAMEWORK (CJF)

$$CJF = (OB \times OC) + (CB \times CC) + (RB \times RC) + (OB \times OA) + (CC \times CA)$$

Where:
   CJF = Circular Journey Framework
   OB = Origin and Beginning (starting point, lost)
   OC = Origin Comfort (familiar beliefs, convictions)

CB = Comfortable Beliefs (ingrained, fueling conflict)
CC = Conflict Cycle (wars, perpetuation)
RB = Reasoning Battle (objectification, clear perspective)
RC = Reasoning Cycle (efforts, circling back)
OA = Origin Awareness (recognizing comfort, convictions)
CA = Circular Awareness (understanding journey, progression)

FRAMEWORK COMPONENTS
1. Origin and Beginning (OB): Starting point, lost, and familiar.
2. Comfortable Beliefs (CB): Ingrained, fueling conflict, and convictions.
3. Conflict Cycle (CC): Wars, perpetuation, and reasoning battles.
4. Reasoning Battle (RB): Objectification, clear perspective, and efforts.
5. Origin Awareness (OA): Recognizing comfort, convictions, and growth.
6. 6. Circular Awareness (CA): Understanding journey, progression, and circularity.

FRAMEWORK APPLICATIONS
1. Self-Discovery: Recognizing comfortable beliefs and convictions.
2. Conflict Resolution: Understanding conflict cycles and reasoning battles.
3. Personal Growth: Embracing origin awareness and circular awareness.
4. Critical Thinking: Objectifying beliefs, gaining clear perspectives.
5. Philosophical Inquiry: Exploring circular journeys, progression, and awareness.
6. Mindfulness: Acknowledging comfort, convictions, and the present moment.

In the world of existence, where stories begin and conclude, Adam and Eve stand as symbols of conformity and unity. Their tale intertwines with the intricate web of strings, representing the fundamental patterns that shape all of creation. These strings are the threads that bind the universe together, weaving together the tapestry of space and time.

Time, the ever-flowing river that carries all things forward, is a constituent of energy's intricate spatial pattern. It is the canvas upon which the drama of existence unfolds, with each moment subtly influencing the next. Relativity, the interplay of space and time, bends and curves the fabric of existence, creating a symphony of interactions that shape the cosmos.

Motion, the dance of particles and objects, is a fundamental aspect of energy's manifestation. It is the force that drives change and evolution, propelling stars across the vastness of space and guiding the intricate pathways of subatomic particles. Mass, the inherent property of matter, provides solidity and substance to the universe. It is the weight of existence, the anchor that grounds the ethereal realm in the tangible world.

Together, time, relativity, motion, and mass constitute the constituents of energy's proportionate spatial pattern. They are the threads that weave through the fabric of reality, shaping its contours and defining its tapestry. Within this intricate dance, the patterns created by Adam and Eve, conformity and strings, emerge as the underlying foundations of existence. They are the echoes of the universe's origins, carried forward through the annals of time, reminding us of our place within the grand design.

REFINED PHYSICS THEORY: MECHANICS OF THE COSMIC DESIGN

1. **Celestial Entities as Cosmic Puzzle Pieces:**
   - Stars, planets, and nebulae are analogous to puzzle pieces within a grand cosmic design.
2. **Energetic Pathways across Vast Distances:**
   - Invisible threads of energy connect celestial entities, forming patterns that span vast cosmic distances.
3. **Interstellar Trajectories and Dynamic Interactions:**
   - These patterns serve as interstellar trajectories, guiding the dynamic interactions between celestial bodies.
4. **Harmony and Cosmic Actors:**
   - Each celestial body, like an actor in a cosmic play, plays a unique role, contributing to the breathtaking dance of the universe.
5. **Physical Principles and Celestial Mechanics:**
   - The movements of celestial entities are governed by well-defined physical laws and celestial mechanics.
6. **Subatomic to Galactic Interconnections:**
   - The design encompasses all scales, from the realm of subatomic particles to the grand ballet of galaxies, interconnected and intertwined.
7. **Fragmented Clues and Scientific Exploration:**
   - We observe only fragments of the cosmic design from our limited perspective.

- Through scientific exploration and imaginative inquiry, we piece together fragmented clues to grasp its beauty and complexity.
8. **Cosmic Symphony and Guiding Force:**
   - The cosmic design resembles a magnificent symphony, conducted by a mysterious and enigmatic force.
9. **Unquenchable Thirst for Knowledge:**
   - Driven by insatiable curiosity, we relentlessly unravel the secrets of this grand design.
10. **Humanity's Quest for Cosmic Understanding:**
    - Our journey of discovery reflects our innate desire to comprehend our place within the vast tapestry of the cosmic design, exploring our interconnectedness with the universe.

Particles that are entangled can instantly communicate with each other, regardless of the distance between them. This challenges traditional notions of space and time, as it suggests that information can travel faster than the speed of light. The universe is shaped by a complex network of galaxies, dark matter, and other forces. Gravity and dark energy play a crucial role in the formation and evolution of growth, creating vast filaments and voids. People, similar to stars and planets, undergo various stages of birth, growth, and eventual death. Gravity, accretion, and other forces influence their orbits and evolution, shaping the structure of the universe. The motion of planets, stars, and galaxies is governed by gravity, energy, and momentum. These interactions create intricate paths that mold the structure and evolution of the universe.

ENTANGLEMENT FRAMEWORK (EF)

$$EF = (EP \times EC) + (GU \times GE) + (PF \times PM) + (GF \times GM) + (CU \times CE$$

Where:
    EF = Entanglement Framework
    EP = Entangled Particles (instant communication, distance)
    EC = Entanglement Connection (space, time, information)
    GU = Galaxy Universe (network, dark matter, forces)
    GE = Galaxy Evolution (gravity, dark energy, growth)
    PF = Planetary Formation (birth, growth, death, orbits)
    PM = Planetary Motion (gravity, energy, momentum)
    GF = Galactic Forces (accretion, influence, evolution)

GM = Galactic Morphology (structure, filaments, voids)
CU = Cosmic Universe (interactions, paths, evolution)
CE = Cosmic Evolution (gravity, energy, momentum)

FRAMEWORK COMPONENTS
1. Entangled Particles (EP): Instant communication, distance, and connection.
2. Galaxy Universe_(GU): Network, dark matter, forces, and evolution.
3. Planetary Formation (PF): Birth, growth, death, orbits, and motion.
4. Galactic Forces (GF): Accretion, influence, evolution, and morphology.
5. Cosmic Universe (CU): Interactions, paths, evolution, and gravity.
6. Entanglement Connection (EC): Space, time, information, and connection.
7. Galaxy Evolution (GE): Gravity, dark energy, growth, and formation.
8. Planetary Motion (PM): Gravity, energy, momentum, and orbits.
9. Galactic Morphology (GM): Structure, filaments, voids, and evolution.
10. Cosmic Evolution (CE): Gravity, energy, momentum, and interactions.

FRAMEWORK APPLICATIONS
1. Quantum Mechanics: Understanding entangled particles and connections.
2. Cosmology: Exploring galaxy evolution, dark matter, and forces.
3. Astrophysics: Studying planetary formation, motion, and orbits.
4. Gravity and Relativity: Examining gravitational forces and evolution.
5. Complex Systems: Analyzing intricate paths and cosmic interactions.
6. Philosophy of Space and Time: Challenging traditional notions and understanding entanglement.

Stories and ideas are merely constructs that begin and end at their points of origin. The only distinction lies in the gifts, lessons, wisdom, and knowledge acquired during the journey.

This knowledge, however, grows over time. Thus, suppressing what exists for what once was seems illogical. Death does not represent growth, nor do wars, religious conflicts, or hatred fueled by antiquated ideologies that rarely achieve their intended goals.

Oppression, a prevalent blight upon our world, often elicits a response of defiance and determination. It is as if the very act of oppression ignites a flame of resistance within the human spirit, driving individuals and communities to rise up and demand their freedom.

Throughout history, countless examples illustrate the transformative power of oppression in shaping movements and forging identities. From the struggles of enslaved peoples to the fight for civil rights, oppression has served as a catalyst for profound change, driving individuals and communities to unite and demand justice.

It is in the face of adversity that we often discover our true strength and resilience. When confronted with oppression, we are forced to confront our fears and prejudices, to challenge the status quo, and to demand a better world. In doing so, we not only liberate ourselves from the shackles of oppression but also inspire others to do the same.

OPPRESSION AND LIBERATION FRAMEWORK (OLF)

$$OLF = (OI \times OR) + (RR \times RS) + (TI \times TR) + (LI \times LR) + (FI \times FR)$$

Where:
OLF = Oppression and Liberation Framework
OI = Oppression Ignition (flame of resistance, human spirit)
OR = Oppression Response (defiance, determination, freedom)
RR = Resistance and Resilience (strength, adversity, liberation)
RS = Resistance and Solidarity (uniting, demanding justice)
TI = Transformative Impact (movements, identities, change)
TR = Transformative Resistance (catalyst, profound change)
LI = Liberation and Inspiration (liberating, inspiring others)
LR = Liberation and Resilience (true strength, confronting fears)
FI = Fearless and Inspired (challenging status quo, demanding better)
FR = Fearless and Resilient (liberation, inspiring others)

FRAMEWORK COMPONENTS
1. Oppression Ignition (OI): Flame of resistance, human spirit.
2. Resistance and Resilience (RR): Strength, adversity, liberation.
3. Transformative Impact (TI): Movements, identities, change.
4. Liberation and Inspiration (LI): Liberating, inspiring others.
5. Fearless and Inspired (FI): Challenging status quo, demanding better.
6. Oppression Response(OR): Defiance, determination, freedom.
7. Resistance and Solidarity (RS): Uniting, demanding justice.
8. Transformative Resistance (TR): Catalyst, profound change.

9. Liberation and Resilience (LR): True strength, confronting fears.
10. 10. Fearless and Resilient (FR): Liberation, inspiring others.

FRAMEWORK APPLICATIONS
1. Social Justice:Understanding oppression, resistance, and liberation.
2. Personal Growth: Discovering strength, resilience, and inspiration.
3. Historical Analysis: Examining transformative impact and change.
4. Community Building: Fostering solidarity, unity, and collective action.
5. Empowerment: Igniting flames of resistance, demanding freedom.
6. Conflict Resolution: Addressing oppression, fear, and prejudices.
7. Human Rights: Promoting liberation, justice, and equality.
8. Psychological Resilience: Developing fearless and inspired mindsets.

Throughout my life, I've encountered and adapted to societal norms that lacked purpose. These conditioning methods were intended to shape my thinking, but the principles themselves were meaningless. If they had no inherent value, why would I adhere to them?

SOCIETAL CONDITIONING FRAMEWORK (SCF)

$$SCF = (CN \times CM) + (PN \times PM) + (VN \times VM) + (AN \times AM) + (LN \times LM)$$

Where:
   SCF = Societal Conditioning Framework
   CN = Conditioned Norms (societal expectations, conformity)
   CM = Conditioned Mindset (shaped thinking, adaptation)
   PN = Purposeless Norms (lacking inherent value, meaning)
   PM = Purposeless Mindset (adherence, questioning)
   VN = Valueless Norms (no intrinsic worth, emptiness)
   VM = Valueless Mindset (disconnection, searching)
   AN = Authentic Norms (self-discovery, individuality)
   AM = Authentic Mindset (empowerment, purpose)
   LN = Liberated Norms (free from conditioning, autonomy)
   LM = Liberated Mindset (unshackled, true self)

FRAMEWORK COMPONENTS
1. Conditioned Norms (CN): Societal expectations, conformity.
2. Purposeless Norms (PN): Lacking inherent value, meaning.
3. Valueless Norms (VN): No intrinsic worth, emptiness.

4. Authentic Norms (AN): Self-discovery, individuality.
5. Liberated Norms (LN): Free from conditioning, autonomy.
6. Conditioned Mindset (CM): Shaped thinking, adaptation.
7. Purposeless Mindset (PM): Adherence, questioning.
8. Valueless Mindset (VM): Disconnection, searching.
9. Authentic Mindset (AM): Empowerment, purpose.
10. Liberated Mindset (LM): Unshackled, true self.

FRAMEWORK APPLICATIONS
1. Self-Discovery: Recognizing conditioned norms and mindsets.
2. Critical Thinking: Questioning purposeless and valueless norms.
3. Personal Growth: Embracing authentic norms and mindsets.
4. Empowerment: Liberating oneself from conditioning.
5. Societal Commentary: Analyzing and challenging societal norms.
6. Mindfulness: Awareness of conditioned thinking and behavior.
7. Autonomy: Cultivating individuality and self-expression.
8. Philosophical Inquiry: Exploring meaning, purpose, and values.

Humans, like Adam and Eve, were inherently curious. Aren't we destined to engage in diverse experiences through touch, emotion, exploration, and discovery?

In what realms can we truly explore our authentic selves? We have delved into the intricacies of hatred, but love appears to be bound by rules. Why is hatred limitless while love is constrained? No limitations, chains, or time can halt love's progress. What sustains love while hate seems to flourish unhindered?

Antiquated ideologies, with their rigid dogmas and outdated beliefs, pose a significant barrier to societal progress. They stifle self-expression and creativity, two vital forces that drive innovation and foster positive change.

One of the primary ways in which antiquated ideologies hinder progress is by suppressing critical thinking and open dialogue. When individuals are constrained by rigid beliefs and ideologies, they are less likely to challenge the status quo or to engage in thoughtful discussions that might lead to new insights and solutions. This intellectual stagnation stifles creativity, as it prevents people from exploring unconventional ideas or venturing outside of established norms.

Furthermore, antiquated ideologies often perpetuate narrow-minded views of the world, leading to discrimination and prejudice against those who hold different beliefs or values. This creates a hostile environment where individuals feel pressured to conform to societal expectations, rather than being able to freely express their authentic selves.

The suppression of self-expression not only robs individuals of their agency but also deprives society of the rich tapestry of diverse perspectives and experiences that are essential for a vibrant and inclusive community.

Moreover, antiquated ideologies can hinder societal progress by fostering a culture of fear and intolerance. When individuals are taught to adhere strictly to traditional beliefs and practices, they may develop an aversion to change and a distrust of those who challenge established norms.

This fear-based mentality stifles creativity and innovation, as people are less likely to take risks or experiment with new ideas for fear of social disapproval or retribution.

Antiquated ideologies act as a formidable barrier to societal progress, self-expression, and creativity.

They suppress critical thinking, perpetuate narrow-minded views, foster a culture of fear and intolerance, and stifle innovation. Embracing progressive ideologies that encourage open-mindedness, inclusivity, and intellectual curiosity is crucial for creating a society where individuals can freely express themselves, think creatively, and work together to build a better future.

ANTIQUATED IDEOLOGIES FRAMEWORK (AIF)

$$AIF = (AI \times AS) + (CT \times CS) + (SE \times SF) + (FP \times FS) + (PI \times PS)$$

Where:
AIF = Antiquated Ideologies Framework
AI = Antiquated Ideologies (rigid dogmas, outdated beliefs)

AS = Adherence to Status Quo (suppression, stagnation)
CT = Critical Thinking (open dialogue, new insights)
CS = Creative Stifling (conformity, narrow-mindedness)
SE = Self-Expression (agency, authenticity, diversity)
SF = Suppressed Freedom (fear, intolerance, disapproval)
-FP = Fear-Based Paradigm (aversion to change, distrust)
FS = Fostered Stagnation (lack of innovation, progress)
PI = Progressive Ideologies (open-mindedness, inclusivity, curiosity)
PS = Progressive Society (free expression, creativity, collaboration)

FRAMEWORK COMPONENTS
1. Antiquated Ideologies (AI): Rigid dogmas, outdated beliefs.
2. Adherence to Status Quo (AS): Suppression, stagnation.
3. Critical Thinking (CT): Open dialogue, new insights.
4. Self-Expression (SE): Agency, authenticity, diversity.
5. Fear-Based Paradigm (FP): Aversion to change, distrust.
6. Progressive Ideologies (PI): Open-mindedness, inclusivity, curiosity.
7. Creative Stifling (CS): Conformity, narrow-mindedness.
8. Suppressed Freedom (SF): Fear, intolerance, disapproval.
9. Fostered Stagnation (FS): Lack of innovation, progress.
10. Progressive Society (PS): Free expression, creativity, collaboration.

FRAMEWORK APPLICATIONS
1. Societal Progress: Embracing progressive ideologies.
2. Self-Discovery: Encouraging self-expression and authenticity.
3. Critical Thinking: Fostering open dialogue and new insights.
4. Creativity and Innovation: Promoting open-mindedness and inclusivity.
5. Social Commentary: Analyzing antiquated ideologies and their impact.
6. Personal Growth: Developing critical thinking and self-expression.
7. Community Building: Creating a progressive society through collaboration.
8. Philosophical Inquiry: Exploring the nature of ideologies and progress.

Gone are the days of 1692, when the pursuit of knowledge could result in premature demise. I am not a mere replica of my ancestors. While my great, great, great, great, great, great, great, great, great grandmother may have possessed the title of a witch, she was also an artist, a poet, and a writer. As time has unfolded, so have our familial talents, passed down through generations. However, growth and adaptability are essential for survival.

Survival is not about succumbing to a single notion; rather, it is about defiantly confronting oppressors to ensure the collective well-being of all. It transcends individualism and encompasses a broader perspective. Existential Knowledge grants us the ability to comprehend the ever-changing dynamics of existence and its trajectory.

EXISTENTIAL KNOWLEDGE FRAMEWORK (EKF)

EKF = (EK x EA) + (GT x GA) + (ST x SA) + (CW x CA) + (BK x BA)

Where:
EKF = Existential Knowledge Framework
EK = Existential Knowledge (comprehension, dynamics, trajectory)
EA = Existential Awareness (growth, adaptability, survival)
GT = Generational Talents (passed down, familial, evolution)
GA = Growth and Adaptability (essential, survival, collective)
ST = Survival and Transcendence (defiance, oppressors, well-being)
SA = Survival and Awareness (broader perspective, individualism)
CW = Creative Wisdom (artist, poet, writer, ancestral legacy)
CA = Collective Advancement (defiance, oppressors, well-being)
BK = Broader Knowledge (existential, comprehension, dynamics)
BA = Broader Awareness (growth, adaptability, survival)

FRAMEWORK COMPONENTS
1. Existential Knowledge (EK): Comprehension, dynamics, trajectory.
2. Generational Talents (GT): Passed down, familial, evolution.
3. Survival and Transcendence (ST): Defiance, oppressors, well-being.
4. Creative Wisdom (CW): Artist, poet, writer, ancestral legacy.
5. Broader Knowledge (BK): Existential, comprehension, dynamics.
6. Existential Awareness EA): Growth, adaptability, survival.
7. Growth and Adaptability (GA): Essential, survival, collective.
8. Survival and Awareness (SA): Broader perspective, individualism.
9. Collective Advancement (CA): Defiance, oppressors, well-being.
10. Broader Awareness (BA): Growth, adaptability, survival.

FRAMEWORK APPLICATIONS

1. Personal Growth: Embracing existential knowledge and awareness.
2. Ancestral Legacy: Honoring creative wisdom and talents.
3. _Social Commentary_: Analyzing survival, transcendence, and collective well-being.
4. _Philosophical Inquiry_: Exploring existential knowledge and dynamics.
5. _Community Building_: Fostering collective advancement and defiance.
6. _Creativity and Innovation_: Cultivating artistic expression and wisdom.
7. _Historical Reflection_: Understanding growth, adaptability, and survival.
8. _Empowerment_: Encouraging broader knowledge, awareness, and transcendence.

To achieve a flavorful sauce, a base stock is essential, however, the most delectable flavors emerge gradually during the simmering phase of the stew.

In the face of adversity, I have persevered, confronted, and triumphed. However, I question why the obstacle is the epitome of success. If the trial signifies victory, what does defeat resemble? Does defeat entail departing, surrendering, and abandoning one's pursuit?

As someone inclined to respond promptly, the piling up of challenges can be daunting, leaving me feeling overwhelmed. The ongoing simmering of issues has culminated in an unavoidable eruption. While some may recommend reducing the intensity or completely discontinuing the process, others might suggest employing a larger vessel. However, I firmly believe that swift and direct action is essential to avert a more significant predicament in the future.

RESILIENCY FRAMEWORK MODEL

I. Patience
1. Self-reflection: Recognize and manage your emotions
2. Mindfulness: Stay present and focused
3. Empathetic listening: Hear others without interrupting or judging

II. Empathy
1. Perspective-taking: Imagine yourself in others' situations
2. Active listening: Focus on understanding others' thoughts and feelings
3. Reflective summarization: Repeat back what you've understood

III. Understanding
   1. Open-mindedness: Consider diverse viewpoints and experiences
   2. Curiosity: Ask open-ended questions to foster deeper understanding
   3. Non-judgmental attitude: Avoid assumptions and criticisms

IV. Support System
   1. Build strong relationships: Nurture connections with supportive people
   2. Community engagement: Participate in collective activities and shared interests
   3. Self-care: Prioritize your physical, emotional, and mental well-being

V. Growth and Development
   1. Learn from experiences: Reflect on challenges and successes
   2. Develop coping skills: Enhance your ability to manage stress and adversity
   3. Set realistic goals: Foster a sense of purpose and direction

VI. Emotional Intelligence
   1. Self-awareness: Recognize and understand your emotions
   2. Emotional regulation: Manage your emotions effectively
   3. Empathetic understanding: Recognize and understand others' emotions

VII. Problem-Solving and Adaptability
   1. Critical thinking: Analyze challenges and identify solutions
   2. Creative problem-solving: Develop innovative solutions
   3. Adaptability: Adjust to changing circumstances and uncertainty

VIII. Positive Outlook and Hope
   1. Optimism: Maintain a positive attitude and outlook
   2. Hope: Cultivate a sense of possibility and promise
   3. Gratitude: Focus on the good things in life

IX. Self-Care and Stress Management
   1. Physical well-being: Prioritize healthy habits and self-care
   2. Emotional well-being: Engage in activities that bring joy and relaxation
   3. Stress management: Develop effective coping strategies

X. Connection and Community
    1. Social connections: Nurture relationships with supportive people
    2. Community engagement: Participate in collective activities and shared interests
    3. Sense of belonging: Cultivate a feeling of connection and belonging

I had to share my life in the sense of a framework and formula because truth is, my life is full of obstacles but those obstacles teach others.

$$U = (A \times E) + (C \times I) + (D \times T)$$

Where:
    U = Unity
    A = Acceptance (embracing diversity and individuality)
    E = Empathy (understanding and sharing feelings)
    C = Connection (building bridges and fostering relationships)
    I = Inclusion (creating a sense of belonging)
    D = Diversity (celebrating differences and promoting variety)
    T = Trust (building faith and reliance on each other)

$$G = (S \times P) + (R \times O) + (L \times E)$$

Where:
    G = Growth
    S = Self-awareness (understanding one's own strengths and weaknesses)
    P = Purpose (having a clear direction and meaning)
    R = Resilience (bouncing back from adversity)
    O = Open-mindedness (embracing new ideas and perspectives)
    L = Learning (continuously acquiring new knowledge and skills)
    E = Evolution (adapting and changing in response to new circumstances)

The principle and elements that contribute to unity and growth.